THE Parenting BREAKTHROUGH

THE Parenting BREAKTHROUGH

A REAL-LIFE PLAN TO TEACH YOUR KIDS TO WORK, SAVE MONEY, AND BE TRULY INDEPENDENT

Merrilee Browne Boyack

DESERET
BOOK

Salt Lake City, Utah

Interior illustrations © 2005 Aaron Taylor.

Library of Congress Cataloging-in-Publication Data

Boyack, Merrilee Browne.
   The parenting breakthrough : real-life plan to teach kids to work, save money, and be truly independent / Merrilee Browne Boyack.
      p.   cm.
   Includes index.
   ISBN-13 978-1-59038-441-1 (pbk.)
1. Parenting—Handbooks, manuals, etc. 2. Child rearing—Handbooks, manuals, etc. I. Title.

HQ755.8.B695 2005
649'.1—dc22   2005002314

Printed in the United States of America
R. R. Donnelley

20   19   18   17   16   15   14

To my daddy, Roger J. Browne Jr. The Great,
who taught me to "Never, never, never give up!"
Probably the best parenting advice ever given.

Contents

Contents

Acknowledgments

I'd like to say thank you to my husband, who nagged me for three years to get this written and has already started bugging me about the next book. I'd like to thank my children who, when I told them I was writing a parenting book, did not burst out laughing and question my sanity. Grateful appreciation also goes to my parents, who did not roll their eyes—at least not in front of me. Thanks also goes to my girlfriends Diane, Sue and Libby, who actually know my children and haven't laughed either but have joined in the nagging with my husband. Thank you to my dog and the two hamsters, who have been the only other females in the household.

Actually, I really do want to thank my parents for much more than not rolling their eyes. They were excellent parents and taught me by actually doing. I'm still blown away that dinner was always on the table by 6:00 P.M. And my husband is absolutely *the* best father on the entire planet. I am not exaggerating. I get choked up whenever I think about how lucky I was to get such a fine dad for these boys. And lots of love goes to my in-laws, who behave as if they think their daughter-in-law walks on water. I've so appreciated their unfailing love. Thank you also

Acknowledgments

to my older sister Kathe, who is about the finest mother I've ever seen and sets such a great example for me.

And thanks to Emily Watts, my editor, who actually encouraged me to include my personality in the book. So if parts of this book seem really weird, you can blame her.

CHAPTER 1

introduction: "Enter to Learn, Go Forth to Serve"

Every time I go to Provo, Utah, and see the words "Enter to Learn, Go Forth to Serve" at the entrance to the Brigham Young University campus, a thrill runs through me. What a lofty purpose! Enter to learn and then use the knowledge you have gained by going forth to serve.

That phrase also describes what we do in our families. We enter into our mortal experience as tiny babies who know nothing. We're here to learn. As parents, we have gone through our initial learning and now have gone forth to serve. Our job is to teach our children so that they, too, are equipped to go forth and serve in the Kingdom. What a beautiful cycle of learning and service! This book will focus on teaching and training our children so that their learning will be effective and complete.

I just need to warn you at the outset that this isn't your usual parenting book. I decided to write this as if I was chatting with my best friend, so it will be a bit different.

Okay, let's start with the *who*. Hello. I'm Merrilee Boyack, and my husband, Steve, and I live in the San Diego, California, area (paradise on earth!). Isn't *Merrilee* a cool first name? My mom chose it because I was born on the twelfth day of Christmas. I have four sons, ages 14, 16, 18, and 23. You know what that means: I am an absolute expert on raising children age 24 and older.

I'm also an attorney. I heard that—you just went, "euuwww." I knew you would. But I run my law practice part-time from home, and in the meantime I do lots of stuff just like you. I'm not a psychologist or anything like that. I'm a mom who has spent the last 23 years in the real-life work of parenting.

Now, on to the *why*. Why did I write this book? Well, when I had my children, I began watching other parents to see what worked and what didn't work. I realized a shocking thing: Very few parents actually had a plan for how they were raising their children. That seemed strange to me. So I developed my own plan. Over the years, many, many people have requested a copy of our family's plan, wanting to know how it works. So here we are!

There are things in this book that you will think are absolutely fabulous and you will implement them immediately and they will change your life. There are some things that you might think are good ideas but not for right now. If you're over 40, you'll forget those things within about 15 minutes, so don't give the book away. If you're under 35, you're probably sleep-deprived with young children, so you'll forget them too. That's okay. Just reread the book—say, every year—and it'll be different for you every time.

And some of the ideas in the book you'll think are incredibly stupid and you are sure you would *never* want to do them. Ah, be very careful. I will now share with you Parenting Tip #1: *Never* say "Never!" I can almost promise you that the minute you get that word past your lips, you will have set in motion a chain of events guaranteeing that you will face that situation. It's a little like having someone dump a bucket of freezing cold water over your head—you don't know whether to be shocked or angry or both. For instance, I can remember looking condescendingly at parents with wild little boys and thinking smugly (with my one docile little boy) that I would *never* have an out-of-control child like that. And of course, my next son was a little hellion whom we lovingly called "J.T." (Junior Terrorist) until he was old enough to realize those were not his initials.

Frankly, I think the Lord starts to chuckle the minute we say, "I would *never* . . ." and He sends us that very challenge. I sometimes wonder if He does it for the sheer entertainment value. I can remember many: "I would *never* feed my children sugary cereals." Or "I would NEVER allow my kids to_____." Feel free to fill in the blank on that one. It is much safer just to avoid the word altogether. Don't even say, "Okay, I will *never* say never!" because that too will backfire. Just a little tip.

Now that you know the *who* and the *why* for me, let me ask you one question: Why are you reading this book? Perhaps you are totally desperate and at your wits' end as to how to handle a particular child or situation. Or perhaps you just like to look around for other good ideas out there that might help you improve. Or maybe your mother-in-law gave you the book with a knowing nod and said, "You better read this—fast!" Whatever the reason, I hope it will be of help to you.

Feel free to pick out the parts that work for you and ignore the others . . . for now. On one condition. We must all take the "Dump the Guilt" pledge. You see, parenting is riddled with guilt. We feel guilty, sure that we're scarring our kids for life, if we don't have dinner on the table at 6:00 every night. We feel guilty if our kids aren't perfect little angels. You're going to read stuff here that makes you think, "Oh, brother, why didn't I do this sooner?" Let it go. Let it all go. You see, you can't do a thing about the past, and all you'll do by worrying about it is get wrinkles.

I have made mistakes as a parent. What? No! Oh please,

we've all made mistakes and we'll keep making them. And as soon as we figure it all out, the kids will leave home.

So let's all dump the guilt about the past and just focus on today and the future. And I will make you a promise. I will try to be very real and very honest. You will not read here that the Boyacks are the perfect family. I can't tell you the number of times my mom would say, "Why don't you have the kids sing? They could perform like the Osmonds." And I'd answer, "Mom, have you heard my kids sing? It could make people cry, and I don't mean that in a good way." So, you'll hear guts, feathers, and all. And don't worry, I've let the family read this book first and have edited as requested.

And while we're making promises, let's add a little caution. I know that mostly moms are reading this book. The dads are getting the filtered version. You know how it goes. You're reading this book and you're saying, "Honey, listen to this." And you read a part. After about the third "sharing," his eyes will glaze over and he'll say, "Honey, if I had wanted to read that book, I would have bought it." So be careful. Read the whole thing and highlight those parts you want to share and then spread them out, like over a month or so, at random moments.

Let me also clarify what this book is *not*. It is not a book to help you with discipline problems and behavioral problems. Many of the principles we discuss will help you with those concerns, but that is not my primary purpose. *This* is a book to help you raise and train children to be independent.

Let me give you an overview of where we're headed so you can get a sense of what's going to be covered. That will satisfy all the to-do list junkies out there—you know who you are. Chapter 2 will discuss the philosophy of raising independent children. This will cover some basic approaches to parenting and some rather crucial mind-sets you need to have in order to parent successfully. It will answer the question of why we're doing the things we do as parents.

Chapter 3 gets pretty exciting, in my own humble opinion, because I'll introduce you to "The Plan." Chapter 4 will talk about some methods to use in parenting with The Plan to accomplish your goals, including how to get your kids to work! These two chapters will discuss how to have a plan for *training* your children, not just making them work. We will focus on life skills and also will discuss several ways to get children to help out with work at home (beyond chore charts), and how to modify these methods as the children get older and won't work for stickers anymore. I know the temptation is great to just jump off the train there, but resist. If you don't know the *why,* the *how* will not be nearly as effective.

Chapter 5 will talk about teaching children about money— exposing the "ATM Makes Money" myth. This is one of the most neglected areas of parenting, with some of the most harmful impacts. Children need to learn to manage their money, and we will explore everything from allowances to jobs. Chapter 6 will take us deeper into financial training, from saving to investing to borrowing. We'll be discussing the practical how-to's involved in the process and trying to make it easier.

Chapter 7 will discuss how to use your family setting to accomplish your parenting goals and how to adapt The Plan to meet your family's needs.

Chapter 8 shares some concepts about the emotional and spiritual development of your family. It will help you talk to your kids and transfer those values that are so important to every parent. We'll explore how to help your kids feel the Spirit and develop testimonies and emotional strength of their own.

Chapter 9 will talk about your parenting philosophy, and we'll review some necessary skills for making it work well.

So grab a bag of cookies or chips or ice cream, prop your feet up, and we'll have a chat!

CHAPTER 2

The Why is As important As the How

I don't know about you, but somebody played a terrible trick on me. Someone just gave me these kids with no instructions. I will never forget having the nurse hand me my first baby in the hospital and thinking, "Now what do I do?" I can remember this terrifying realization that I had to take him home and take care of him, and I didn't know how to do that. It had been a long time since I was even a baby-sitter. It was scary, to say the least.

Well, by the time they handed me my second baby, I thought, "No sweat. I know what to do." Except there was a mean trick: Child #2 was *nothing* like child #1. And this trick has been repeated. By the time the fourth baby came, I just looked at him and thought, "Well, let's find out who you are, and we'll learn this together."

Obviously, someone forgot to give me the Parenting Owner's Manual. I mean, if I buy a stereo, they give me a manual. If I get a computer, there are tons of manuals. If I purchase a car, I certainly get a manual. But you acquire something as important as a child, and *she doesn't come with a manual*. Big problem.

So you have this child, and you don't have a clue what to do. And yet you know that bringing this child up is probably the most important thing you'll ever do. Isn't that quite a dilemma?

Lacking a better alternative, we begin with trial and error—and that's basically how we do the whole thing. We read a little, pick up what we can, and pray an awful lot.

My first son loved to sit and read in my lap. So I take my second son, sit him in my lap, and begin to read. Screaming child in 0.2 nanoseconds. Okay, that didn't work. I'll try something else. To get my second son to do something, I would say, "I'm counting to five." He'd put his hands over his ears and yell, "Don't count! Don't count!!" He couldn't stand it and felt compelled to do the required task before I reached the end. Aha! That worked like a charm—he was a compulsive numbers boy.

So with child #3 I say, "I'm going to count to five." He just looks at me and says, "Okay, go ahead." It didn't work *at all*. I had to start from scratch learning what would work with him. And on it went.

And that's not all. The mean trick continued. Counting worked great with child #2—when he was a little child. Now that he's 18, it doesn't work at all. So not only am I coping with different kids, but they change every year and even minute by minute sometimes. It's like waking up every day and finding a new computer sitting on your desk. How are you supposed to keep up with that?

And so, *this* is parenting. Trial and error. Hanging in there. And an infinite amount of patience. Basically, I think the whole thing is an exercise in patience designed to help us become more like God.

Purposes of Parenting

Let's get down to the basic philosophy of parenting. I like to divide it into three primary purposes or tasks:
1. Health and safety of children
2. Values education

3. Training children to be independent adults

It's our job as parents to keep our children as healthy and safe as we can. So we teach them to look before they cross the street, eat their vegetables, and avoid strangers. We take them to the doctor and dentist and try to protect them from physical harm.

It's also our job to pass on the values and character traits that are important to us. We teach them about God and the purpose of life. We teach them about how to be honest, how to be friendly, and so on. This is a crucial part of our job as parents, one that we simply cannot abdicate.

Finally, it's our job to train our children to be independent so they are capable of moving on and creating families of their own. This is true of the whole animal kingdom: You see the mommy and daddy birds, bears, or whatever teaching their offspring how to eat, care for themselves, and stay safe so they can grow up to be on their own.

It is fascinating that, as important as this third purpose of parenting is, many parents are failing abominably at it. You don't see the mommy and daddy bear saying, "Well, gee, kids. We can see it's a big, scary world out there. Why don't all of you just keep hanging out in the cave with us." No way. They teach them well and then boot them out.

As I was beginning my parenting, I observed an interesting phenomenon. I saw many young adults living at home and the parents making excuses as to why they were still there. It was incredible. I would ask, "Well, were things cheap when you first moved out on your own?" And of course, they would tell me all their stories of how they ate on a card table and scrimped and saved to be able to get a house. And yet, they don't see things the same way for their children.

And let's face it, many of these young adults truly are incapable of taking care of themselves because they've been

raised to be dependent leeches. This is called the Boomerang Phenomenon—adult children coming back (or staying) home with their parents.

I don't want to give offense to anyone, but I want my children to grow up and *move away* so I can have grandchildren I can visit! Isn't that why we had children to begin with? I want the icing on the cake. Not only do I want lots of grandchildren, but I want to spend years watching my children raise them. Talk about joy. I don't think it can get any better than that. I want to listen to my kids complaining about how their children won't clean their rooms, won't do what they're told, and are lazy and unmotivated. I'm going to spend decades just laughing. My grandkids are going to think they have the happiest grandma on the planet.

And might I say just a small thank you at this point to my mother? She has not once laughed out loud in front of me. Frankly, I think she's rather horrified by it all. She had only one docile son who was the baby in the family, and being in the presence of our four—enthusiastic—boys (wasn't that a kind choice of words?) drives her to her bed.

Anyway, my husband and I realized early on that it was critical to rear our children to be fully capable of getting caves of their own. John Rosemond, one of my absolutely favorite parenting authors, sums it up nicely, "The ultimate goal of raising children is to help them out of our lives and into successful lives of their own" (*John Rosemond's Daily Guide to Parenting* [Sta-kris, 1994], Oct. 10).

Americans are raising a generation of children "with extremely low levels of competence in domestic skills," according to two sociologists, Linda Waite of the University of Chicago and Frances Goldscheider of Brown University. "Teenage boys do about the same as toddler boys . . . that's almost nothing. We call them free riders." Two reasons are cited: one, that we're taking our kids to soccer games rather than doing chores; and two, "There's a training component to many chores; you have to show kids how to make a salad or bake cookies," says Waite. "Sometimes, it's just easier to do the chores ourselves" (Betty Holcomb, "Life Skills 101," *Good Housekeeping,* May 1, 2000).

The real problem with doing everything ourselves is that we end up always doing everything ourselves. And our children don't grow up; they just get bigger.

President James E. Faust commented on this important parental duty: "Children need to learn responsibility and independence. Are the parents personally taking the time to show and demonstrate and explain so that children can, as Lehi taught, 'act for themselves and not . . . be acted upon'? (2 Ne. 2:26.) . . .

"There is often a special challenge for those parents who are affluent or overly indulgent. In a sense, some children in those circumstances hold their parents hostage by withholding their support of parental rules unless the parents acquiesce to the children's demands. Elder Neal A. Maxwell has said, 'Those who do too much *for* their children will soon find they can do nothing *with* their children. So many children have been so much *done for* they are almost *done in'*" ("The Greatest Challenge in the World—Good Parenting," *Ensign*, November 1990, 33–34).

Nurturing Vs. Training

Our parenting must be balanced. Too much nurturing will cripple our children. Don't be shocked! Think about this for a minute. Overnurturing is like giving too much fertilizer or too much water to plants. The plants don't develop deep roots. They just stay shallow because they're being lavished with too much of a good thing.

We see lots of this around, this "Martyr Mom Syndrome." Do you know one of these women? This mom does everything for her children. They are the center of her universe. Sometimes a dad will fall into this category as well. These parents lavish so much nurturing that their kids are drowning in it. What's interesting is that they often get no respect from their children, and they end up walking around with simmering resentment most of the time. When you ask them why they are parenting this way, they say, "I *love* my children. I want them to be happy." Those are dangerous parenting words. "What?" you ask. "Isn't that how we're all supposed to feel?" Please read on.

Let me share a story of my friend Rose (most names are being changed to protect the innocent and the guilty). My friend also had four sons, about 15 years older than mine. She was an amazing woman—the ultimate homemaker, and Relief Society president in our ward. Her nurturing ways were in absolute hyperdrive. She used to brag that she taught her sons to make their beds when they left for their missions or to go off to college. Wince!

One day we were having a Relief Society presidency meeting at my home, where we met because I had little ones. (Did I mention that the education counselor was also an incredible homemaker? I used to refer to those two as Martha Stewart I and Martha Stewart II. Now, to top that—*I* was the homemaking counselor. As I said, the Lord has a major sense of humor.)

Anyway, we were sitting there in my kitchen and in walked my youngest son, Tanner, who was about three years old. He went over to the pantry and got out the peanut butter, the jelly, and the bread. Then he very carefully laid the bread out on the floor and proceeded to make himself a sandwich. I could see him out of the corner of my eye and I didn't do a thing. I could also see the other women, MS I and II, developing serious facial twitches and jumping about in their chairs. Finally Rose couldn't stand it. She said, "Merrilee! Your son is making a sandwich on the bare floor!" I responded, "I know. Isn't that fantastic! He just learned how to make sandwiches this week." And I turned to Tanner and with a big smile said, "Tanner, I am *so* proud of you. What a yummy sandwich you've made!" He was positively beaming with pride and joy as he walked out with his sandwich. I think poor MS I and MS II aged several years on the spot.

Parents who nurture too much convey messages like these to their children: You can't do this because—

you're not smart enough.

you're not reliable enough.

you're not old enough.

you're not responsible enough.

you're *just* a child.

I don't trust you.

I don't believe in you.

you're not capable of taking care of yourself.

the quality of your work is inadequate.

working is bad.

only women do these kinds of things.

only men do these kinds of things.

moms do all the dirty work [conveying a serious lack of respect for women].

Parents, and especially mothers, who continue to insist on doing things for the children that they are capable of doing on their own convey these messages constantly. I know that such parents are well-intentioned and think they are showing love and caring, but they are damaging their children in the process because they are not looking at the big picture.

Some of these Overdrive Nurturers think that they are communicating love by continuing to do these things. What is interesting is that they often end up raising children who treat them like the doormats they've become. Then these parents wonder how they raised such selfish, greedy monsters.

Is this how we show love best? By communicating our children's incompetence and training them to be self-centered beasties? For that is absolutely what these parents are doing—they are *training* their children to be this way. They have been training them since Day 1 that Mom or Dad or both will do all their work and that the universe revolves around them. Small wonder that the kids don't want to leave home, for the world has the opposite viewpoint. This is why I said it was dangerous to say, "But I *love* my children." If we show that love by constant showering—*drenching*—with attention, praise, and material goods, making the children the center of the world, they believe that and can be permanently damaged by that message.

Some of these nurturers continue on in their ways because they cannot bear to hear their children whine and complain. So they constantly cave in. They place their children's happiness above their own, even if it is temporary. When parents say, "I want my children to be happy," they are usually focused on the short-term.

Case in point is Freida, who had one child. Freida often felt deprived as a youth because she grew up in a home with a frugal mother. She decided when she had a child that she would never tell the child "no." I will never forget talking to her when her son was five. I asked her, "What would you do if he asked for a Corvette?" She replied that she would probably buy him one. It is now fascinating to see this same child at the age of about thirty-five. He can barely function on his own. Mom is still taking care of his bank account and finances. Is he truly happy? No way.

You may consider this quite the extreme. You would *never* do such a thing, right? Remember what I said about "never" being dangerous? Many parents are communicating exactly the same idea when they give in all the time. They are saying, "Well, I'll say *no,* but if you whine enough and complain enough and wear me down enough, that will change to a *yes.*" Same end result. Remember, here again, the child is being trained.

Contrast this with parents who keep the end in mind while raising their children. These parents truly love their children and want them to be happy. But (and it's a big but) they also understand that sometimes the best way to show their children love is to back off, let them experience life, and—dare I say it—let their children be miserable sometimes.

These parents understand that if they keep their nurturing in check, or better yet, focused, then they can accomplish great things. They can allow their children to learn and then do on their own. They can refuse to do things their children are capable of doing, resisting the whining and complaining that will inevitably occur, and train their children to be independent.

This parental attitude conveys a singularly important message to the child: *"You are valuable and capable and worthwhile."*

Little Tanner felt extremely capable and worthwhile as he trotted off with his dust-covered sandwich. I could have run over, moved everything to the counter, and made him the sandwich myself—a really clean sandwich. And I would have conveyed the message, "You can't do this—you're too little." Which message conveyed love?

It's interesting to watch how children understand and pick up on this. One day my son Parker came home and said, "I feel so sorry for the neighbor girl. Her mom doesn't let her do her own wash." This from a son who was nine years old. I had to hide my smile and commiserate. And I thought, her mom probably feels she is being loving and nurturing by doing all of the laundry for her girls.

Another time we were having a little cooking class in my backyard for the neighbor children (I know you're wondering about that one. It was cooking in a Dutch oven. I can handle the outside cooking thing fairly well—enough so that it is somewhat edible, at least.) Anyway, none of the neighborhood six-year-olds could use the can opener. I had forgotten that most people don't use a manual one. Later my son commented, "I feel sorry for those babies." He felt very grown up because he knew how to use that little appliance.

Three Basic Parenting Principles

Summarizing this line of thought, I believe there are three basic parenting principles we need to embrace to be successful in raising independent children:

Principle #1: You are not responsible for making your children happy all the time.

In fact, that is about the worst thing you can do to your kids. "If you are so determined, you can indeed keep a child happy for eighteen years," says John Rosemond. "In the process, you will surely destroy the child's self-esteem. Why? Because self-esteem is reflected in the child's belief that 'I can do it myself!'" (*Daily Guide to Parenting*, Nov. 26). To raise great kids, we need to let them experience frustration, delayed gratification, sadness, misery, and the host of negative feelings common to mankind. What better place to go through all this than at home? It is a safe environment with parents watching out by protecting the children from really serious difficulties, and they can learn wonderful coping and independence skills.

When children who have been kept perpetually happy move out into the world, they are ill-equipped to deal with the normal frustrations and trials that are part of adult living. At the first sign of difficulty, they'll run crying home to mama to make it all better.

One day I caught my son watching TV when it was not permitted (we allowed it only on weekends), and he looked up at me with those big, puppy-dog eyes and said, "Don't you want me to be happy?" I smiled and said, "No!" He was shocked. I continued, "I want you to be righteous, productive, skilled, smart, helpful, wise, intelligent, and hardworking. *That's* what I want you to be. If you feel happy occasionally, that's cool." I then reassured him that TV was dead last on the list and he could go work off his infraction to build character.

I know this attitude is rather counterintuitive to parents. I mean, isn't it our *job* to make our kids happy? Yes and no. They need regular doses of happiness, but they also need doses of experiencing the trials of real life. We need to look at those negative times with rejoicing instead of guilt feelings. We can say to ourselves, "Yahoo! She's frustrated with that hard school project." "Yay, he has a teacher with a different personality that clashes a bit." Just think of all the wonderful lessons they will learn adapting, coping, adjusting, and so forth. We need to curb our instinct to run in and fix everything and smooth out all of life's wrinkles.

We need to keep the end in mind constantly in order to be able to battle the guilty feelings and the stares of others. What will we do when our child comes to us complaining about sadness? Will we fix it, or will we empower the child with a message like this: "Sweetheart, I know this is really hard but I have every confidence that you can handle it. I've seen you handle tough things before. You can do this!" And then we stand back—with tongues sufficiently bitten when the child chooses differently than we would and hands tied behind our backs to resist fixing things—and we ooze faith and confidence in the child.

Over time our children will learn to make themselves happy. They will learn to choose that state of mind on their own. And we will have been successful parents.

Principle #2: The best self-esteem for children comes from being able to do things on their own.

Ann Landers had wise advice: "In the final analysis it is not what you do for your children but what you have taught them to do for themselves that will make them successful human beings." We are raising a whole generation of children who have no concept of work. They have too much food, too many clothes, too many toys, and they don't have to work for any of it.

We drag our kids from soccer games to dance lessons to karate to Girl Scouts to baseball and on and on. We mistakenly believe that all these things will give our kids high self-esteem. But we need to stop and think this through for a moment. Compare the shiny, plastic gold trophy for playing on the team with the day your child gets her driver's license. Remember how that felt? Why? Because your child knows that she can do something on her own—she can drive a car. And that's a very big, adult thing. I'm not saying that activities for our children are bad. What I'm saying is that such activities are not the great source of self-esteem we all think they are.

Our children will get their best feelings of self-confidence from being independent and capable. Remember how great it felt the first time you got dressed by yourself (think *way* back), or made your own bed, curled your own hair, fixed the car yourself, made dinner for the family? You felt so grown up and able!

"People who see only the economic value of family work miss what some call the 'Invisible Household Production'—the potential of family work to transform lives, to forge strong families, to build strong communities" (Kathleen S. Bahr with Cheri A. Loveless, "Family Work," *Brigham Young Magazine,* Spring 2000). Having our children do things for themselves is what makes them not only grow up but *mature* along the way.

President Gordon B. Hinckley has said: "Work together. I don't know how many generations or centuries ago, someone first said, 'An idle mind is the devil's workshop.' Children need to work with their parents—to wash dishes with them, to mop floors with them, to mow lawns, to prune trees and shrubbery, to paint and fix up and clean up and do a hundred other things where they will learn that labor is the price of cleanliness and progress and prosperity" (*Teachings of Gordon B. Hinckley* [Deseret Book, 1997], 707).

Children lack the maturity to know what's best for them. That's why they have parents. They may think that sitting around or playing all day is the best way to be happy. Parents who have vision know better.

Children perceive adult functions as important and worthwhile. They know that those grown-up activities are of value. And they find such activities very attractive because they want to be mature grown-ups as well. *The best source of true self-esteem will come from your child being able to competently perform adult, independent functions.*

So, recently I was watching a TV show (yes, I do that occasionally) where they were discussing adult children who were still living at home. My two youngest sons were watching with me. It was fascinating to listen to my sons' comments throughout the show: "Man, that guy should go get a job!" "Why do those parents let their kids do that?" "Mom, you should be running that show. You taught us how to work and do all that stuff." But the funniest comment came from Parker at the end of the program: "Brother—*I* could teach this show! You've taught us everything they talked about!" And I realized they were probably right. They *could* have taught it because they knew how to work, they knew how to do adult things, and as a result they had lots of self-confidence.

Frankly, I think the whole "self-esteem" business has been majorly overrated. We have had it so drilled into us our whole lives that now that we are parents, we think it is the biggest part of our parenting. In fact, it is often what stymies us. We think, "Oh dear, I don't want to reprimand little Susie. I might damage her self-esteem!" And so we hesitate from being assertive, in-charge parents. Which leads us to Principle #3 . . .

Principle #3: Remember that we are the parents and we are in charge.

President David O. McKay taught: "The home is the first and most effective place for children to learn the lessons of life: truth, honor, virtue, self-control; the value of education, honest work, and the purpose and privilege of life. Nothing can take the place of home in rearing and teaching children, and no other success can compensate for failure in the home" (*Family Home Evening Manual*, 1968–69, iii).

Overall, our parents' generation did a great job. Their kids respected them and grew up to be self-sufficient adults. Think about it. How often do you find yourself saying to your children something like, "Man, if I had ever said that to my dad, he would have locked me in my room for a week!" We need to recognize that times have changed, of course, but do we feel that the general quality of parenting has improved? I think we could probably agree that our children do not respect us as much on the whole, and they are often not as capable as we were at their ages.

One of the philosophies that has contributed to this is the concept of the child-centered family. I hear comments like these all the time: "Well, we're focused on the children." Or "My kids are everything to me." Can this really work? Think of riding a bicycle. Everything is balanced nicely. Now think of stacking up all your kids and all their stuff, and what happens? The slightest bump in the road, and the whole thing falls over and collapses. Change your thinking now, and picture having a nice tandem bike for you and your spouse. You are leading the way. And each child behind you is on his or her own bike, from the sleek 20-speed to the mountain bike to the cute pink bike with shiny streamers to the little tricycle peddling like mad in the back.

Our role as parents is to provide a solid grounding for the family in the stability and security of our marriage. Then we provide leadership and vision for the family. We need to be comfortable in that leadership role. If we firmly understand and accept our first two parenting principles—that our job is not to make

our kids happy all the time and that true self-esteem comes from capabilities—we will be able to implement this third principle more easily.

So, let's say you're now comfortable with the idea of being in charge. The first challenge will come when your child asks, "Why do I have to?" Our parents were geniuses. They had a short answer: "Because I said so." When your boss gives you an instruction or direction, do you stomp your little feet, bunch up your lips into a pout, and whine, "But *why?*" Not unless you want to be out of a job rather quickly. Because the answer is often, "I have more information than you do and more experience than you do and I understand where we're headed."

As parents, we have to be willing to experience frustration, lack of cooperation, and challenges to our patience and certainly to our sanity, all without giving in! Sometimes I have to go into my room and give myself a little pep talk: "These kids are driving me nuts. Why can't they just do what they know they're supposed to do without griping all the time? But I know where we're headed. I am training independent adults. I am in charge. I can do this." And I pull back my shoulders, lift my head, and head out the door ready to meet the challenge. Of course, that usually ends with my children muttering to themselves that their mother is wacko and that she has *way* too many conversations with herself. But I'm okay with that!

Now, as an "in-charge" parent, you need to take charge. You need to be comfortable in your role as a leader of the home. If your children are constantly challenging you and you are often unsure of your decisions, it might mean that you have not yet really decided to be in charge. Three ideas can help you have more confidence in taking the reins of leadership:

1. You're a lot older! You've got a lot more experience and real-life smarts than your children do. Take confidence in that, and also accept the fact that your children don't understand it and they certainly don't or won't give you credit for it. That doesn't change the reality.

2. You're doing the best you can. I don't know of one single parent who wakes up in the morning saying, "You know, today I'm going to try to be a crummy parent." Baloney. Every day you do the best you can, which is great.

3. You're entitled to the direction of the Spirit. If you are

living a good and worthy life, the Spirit is with you constantly and is directing you in your thoughts and actions more than you will ever know.

If you've struggled with this in the past, today is the day to take charge. You can sit the children all down for a lovely bonding family moment and say, "Kids, we've realized that we haven't been taking a leadership role in our family like we should. We've been giving in to your demands and letting our fatigue take over, and that's wrong. As of today, we want you to know that you can count on us to be in charge of this family."

Oh, just picture it. All your children will leap up and kiss you and hug you and say, "Gee, thanks, Mom and Dad! We're so proud of you and we love you." Yeah, well, let's add a reality check there. They're more likely to look at you in disbelief and probably, if they're old enough, say, "Oh, great! We have the worst parents in the world. You guys are so harsh. What's this supposed to mean to us?" and other similar grumblings.

Congratulations! You've just taken the first great step! Your children don't know it, but you've given them a wonderful gift that will benefit their whole lives. Now go eat some chocolate and take a well-deserved time-out in your room.

CHAPTER 3

"The Plan" for Training Kids to Be independent

As I mentioned in the first chapter, I was shocked to realize that few parents of my acquaintance had an actual overall plan for raising their children. Think about that for a moment. All our lives we're taught to make plans and set goals and to write them down. We have a plan for our education; we have a plan for our career; we have a plan for our homes; and we have tons of plans for how to lose weight. You wouldn't think of going on a family vacation without having at least some idea of where you were going and how long you were going to stay.

And yet, most parents haven't even thought about having a parenting plan, much less actually writing one down. They have a vague idea that they will feed and clothe their children and watch them until they grow big enough that the government says it's legal to send them out on their own. Perhaps somewhere along the line they might teach them a thing or two. But most parents approach parenting on a day-to-day basis with rather amorphous ideas of what to do at that particular time.

Being the rather obsessive-compulsive list maker that I am, I spent several months consulting with my husband on what we wanted to do with our children, and I actually wrote down The

Plan. Over the past 23 years we have modified and adjusted The Plan, but on the whole it has worked amazingly well.

Now that you've actually thought about it, you might want to have a written plan as well. If you like, you can begin with ours and modify as you go along. I call it "The Fabulously Brilliant, Flexible, and Comprehensive Plan for Raising Independent Children Who Will Be Able to Take Care of Themselves as Adults and Have a Family Plan of Their Own." How about if we just call it "The Plan" for short?

To begin with The Plan, you need to start with the end in mind. Think back for a moment to when you first left home, perhaps for college or a mission or a job and apartment. When you moved out, what did you *not* know how to do? What came as a surprise to you? I can remember several things: I had never had a checking account, never taken care of a car, never made my own doctor's appointments, and on and on. I'm sure you could come up with a long list of things that you suddenly had to scramble to learn how to do.

A few years ago my niece Krystal went off to college for her freshman year. She was staying in an apartment with five other girls, and they would all be cooking for themselves. Her mother, my fabulous older sister Kathe, recounted to me an interesting conversation. All the moms were hanging around in the kitchen chatting. Three of the moms said, "Boy, I sure hope my daughter will not starve to death. She doesn't have the slightest idea how to cook." Then the moms began to discuss the things their daughters didn't know how to do and chuckled to think of them having to learn it all. My sister was horrified, as was I. Who did they expect would teach their children how to cook—and when? Let's take a most stressful time in those girls' lives: they're in a strange state, strange city, big school teeming with 30,000 people, apartment with five strangers, and difficult classes. They're supposed to just pick up these skills on their own then?

Or did they think the magical Parenting Fairy would come along and do everything for them?

I recall another friend's daughter who went off to school with a car. After a time the car totally seized up and wouldn't run—on the freeway, no less. Diagnosis: no oil=locked up engine. "What oil?" says the daughter. You see, the Daddy Fairy had dutifully kept the oil filled and changed, not wanting to worry his daughter's pretty little head with such "guy stuff."

Think of the son buying his first car. He goes in and the salesman points to the sticker on the window and says, "That's the price of the car." Boy says, "Okay, I need a loan." Salesman (now with a radiating smile of glee) says "No problem" and signs up Boy with lovely payments lasting through the next century. Boy goes home and tells parents he bought his first car on his own. Dad has a cow and says, "Don't you know only idiots pay the sticker price?" Boy is bewildered. Isn't that the price? It works that way at Wal-Mart and at the mall. No one ever taught him differently.

Think of it this way: We have Mommy Eagle and Daddy Eagle with now Grown-Child Eagle. They take GCE to a cliff, toss him over, and say, "Welcome to Adult Eaglehood, Son! Good luck! Sorry we didn't teach you how to fly!" And yet, day after day children leave home with major, crucial gaps in their training. Some fill in those gaps along the way, often not very well, and others grope along and never catch on their whole lives. It has been intriguing to me in my positions in Relief Society to learn that those women who struggled most with their homes and family were not lazy or stupid. In almost every case, they were the products of poor training by their parents. And often those parents just didn't realize that they didn't know any better. Congratulations—you *will* know better!

Developing a Master Plan

So let's begin with the end in mind. Pull out a piece of paper and write on it, "How I Want My Children to Turn Out." You're probably going to want kids who can care for themselves, keep a job, have good professional and interpersonal skills, and so forth. Now, we all want our children to be rocket scientists with huge bank accounts and fabulous families, but let's be realistic. (I told my kids I needed one plastic surgeon, one mechanic, one dentist, and one travel-industry professional to make my retirement perfect. None of them are cooperating.) Bottom line, what basic things do you want your children to know and be? Write at least five main goals or results.

This part of The Plan is absolutely crucial. You will be spending many hours of many days doing things that seem trivial or pointless, and you have to have that end goal firmly in mind to get yourself through them. So when you're teaching your daughter for the umpteenth time how to thoroughly clean a toilet, you can say to yourself, "We're training an independent adult here. This is important." Besides, just think how desirable your kids will be! Trust me, they'll be irresistible! I already have parents lining up their daughters for my sons because they know they can take care of a car, whip up a meal, garden, and clean that blessed toilet!

With that end in mind, the rest of The Plan flows fairly easily. My husband and I made an incredibly long list of every task we could think of that our children needed to be able to do to get to the end goal of independence. You may start with ours, but don't assume it covers everything. We are constantly adding to our list and modifying it. Feel free to change the list as you work with it—and send me your changes! I had to add all kinds of girl things like "Hair management" that hadn't even occurred to me.

Then we took each of these tasks and assigned it to an age at which we thought the child would be capable of learning it. Keep in mind that every child is different. Some learn things faster and are more motivated. Others would like to just live in the home cave for the rest of their lives and have no motivation to do any of it. So this is a fairly flexible plan. But keep in mind that if more than one or two years slip by, you need to up the ante and get that child trained.

Let's review The Plan and then we'll talk about how it works.

THE PLAN

THREE YEARS OLD
Dress self
Use toilet independently
Beginning to brush teeth
Pick up toys
Say prayers
Clean glass tables

FOUR YEARS OLD
Brush teeth
Make bed
Make own breakfast
Make sandwiches
Beginning to clean room

FIVE YEARS OLD
Straighten room
Vacuum
Empty garbage cans
Set table
Clear table
Make own lunch
Warm up canned food
Get allowance

SIX YEARS OLD
Take shower
Dust
Load dishwasher
Empty dishwasher
Clean sinks
Run microwave
Water plants
Make and answer phone calls

SEVEN YEARS OLD
Wash dishes
Floss teeth
Clean toilets
Pull weeds
Have a savings account
Read with comprehension

EIGHT YEARS OLD
Groom nails and hair
Get up by self
Participate in team sports or
    clubs
Develop personal talents
Clean mirrors

SEVEN YEARS OLD (CONT.)

Memorize phone number and
 address
Do own hair
Begin piano lessons

NINE YEARS OLD

Mop floor
Clean pictures
Bake cakes
Bake cookies
Understand emergency
 preparedness
Learn basic first aid
Fill car with gas
Wash car
Vacuum interior of car
Hammer nails
Saw wood
Cook vegetables
Write letters
Understand puberty and sex
Use e-mail
Understand basic science
Wrap presents
Sew on buttons

ELEVEN YEARS OLD

Arrange for own haircuts
Clean refrigerator
Clean cupboards
Straighten drawers
Straighten closets
Sew hems
Bake pies
Bake bread
Make several main dishes

EIGHT YEARS OLD (CONT.)

Get baptized
Read scriptures daily
Care for pet

TEN YEARS OLD

Do own laundry completely
Set personal goals
Play musical instrument
Maintain personal journal
Participate in exercise
 program
Rent videos
Clean stove
Clean oven
Make several kinds of salad
Understand basic nutrition
Use leaf blower
Plant plants
Place a collect call
Use a pay phone
Place a long-distance call
Know Articles of Faith
Write creatively

TWELVE YEARS OLD

Shop for clothing
Have basic fashion awareness
Plan wardrobe
Develop reading program
Read newspaper
Speak in public
Understand weight control
Make and keep dentist
 appointment

ELEVEN YEARS OLD (CONT.)

Iron own clothes
Plan meals
Mow lawn
Use weed whacker
Maintain garden
Place credit-card call
Start basic mission
  preparation
Have good basic math skills
Use a camera
Learn to crochet or knit
Participate in first aid training
Take a baby-sitting class
Clean windows
Use Internet (filtered!)

THIRTEEN YEARS OLD

Sew simple items
Shop for clothing and other
  items
Find bargains
Plan parties
Have own recipe files
Shop for groceries
Care for plants
Keep a simple budget
Pay household bills
Use ATM
Certify for CPR
Type without looking
Go to movies without parent
Understand prescriptions
Learn meat-handling rules

TWELVE YEARS OLD (CONT.)

Make and keep doctor
  appointment
Keep personal calendar
Understand basic filing
Use common computer
  programs
Order something by phone
Order something by mail
Order something on Internet
Read Book of Mormon
  through
Attend priesthood or Young
  Women activities
Check fluids in car
Paint interior and/or exterior
  of house
Baby-sit
Mend clothing

FOURTEEN AND FIFTEEN
YEARS OLD

Do basic interior decorating
Understand food storage basics
Memorize Social Security
  number
Understand and use debit cards
Learn interest, debt, securities
Learn about makeup (girls!)
Identify business skills to get
  some experience with sales
Learn basic civics and politics
Accompany parent to vote
Perform thorough car detailing
Change flat tire
Understand basics of car
  operation

THIRTEEN YEARS OLD (CONT.)
Learn etiquette rules
Clean garage
Sell items on Internet

SIXTEEN AND SEVENTEEN YEARS OLD
Get driver's license
Understand credit cards
Learn retirement plans
Resume mission preparation
Understand interviewing
Understand advertising
Start career planning
File insurance claim
Arrange for car insurance
Perform household repairs
Assist in purchase of car
Open checking account
File tax return
Deal with auto mechanic
Plan landscaping
Pay for and use cell phone
Get a job

FOURTEEN AND FIFTEEN YEARS OLD (CONT.)
Do simple household repairs
Put up wallpaper
Memorize seminary scriptures

EIGHTEEN YEARS OLD
(OK, a mom can dream!)
Tell parents they're fabulous
Spontaneously quote scriptures in Sunday School
Stop by to visit parents and offer to help
Start buying parents really expensive gifts
Shall I go on? I love dreaming!

Rather incredible, isn't it? We have to know a *lot* before we can be successful adults. You may be thinking as you read through this list, "Gee, *I* still need to learn some of these things." It's never too late!

As I said before, feel free to add to this list all you would like. If you would like an electronic copy of the list, send me an e-mail at maboyack@gmail.com and I'll send it to you. Spend some time both by yourself and with your spouse and family reviewing the list and seeing if anything particular to your family needs to be added. You may certainly want to add some items that fit your own family's spiritual values as well as your family's personality. You may be big sports buffs and not care at all about music. You may love to have your daughters do dance or whatever. Make this list fit who your family is and who your children are.

Implementing The Plan

Okay, so you've got this massive list and you've just entered into a deep depression and are overwhelmed with fatigue just thinking about it. I know that it's rather staggering to look at what we're supposed to train our children to do, but hang in there. You will be amazed at how well this plan will fit into your family and what a difference it will make.

I also want to encourage those of you who have teenagers. You're probably looking at this list thinking, "Oh, brother, I waited too long! Now what shall I do?" Don't worry. We'll get you there.

Let's go through the steps on how to implement this plan, and I'll give you some tips along the way to help you out. Remember, step 1: *dump the guilt!* So what if you never thought about this before? That's okay. Your kids are still functional, and you can start now. That's great!

It's really helpful to introduce your Master Plan in a family meeting. If your children are all babies and toddlers, you can hold the meeting anyway with your spouse. The family meeting will go something like this: "Kids, I'd like to welcome you to our family meeting." [Grumble, complain—oh, sorry, I just had to make this realistic.] "Your dad and I have learned this great plan and we're going to use this in our family." [More griping, "Oh, lovely. Now we're a science experiment . . ."] "So we have a question for you. Would you like to eventually be a successful grown-up and have a home and family of your own?" [Cue teenage son, "I'm never getting married and I'm certainly not having kids." Just keep smiling and keep talking. Little daughter starts crying, "Can't I just stay with you and Daddy?" Hang in there, you're doing great.]

"We figured that you would all like to become mature adults and to be able to take care of yourselves. So we've put together this plan to get you there." Pull out the list and show it to the kids. [Expect exclamations of horror: "Plan meals? I'm not doing that." And also perhaps some positive comments, "Shop for clothing. Right on! How about today?"]

Go over The Plan with the kids so they see what it is. Talk repeatedly about *why* you're doing this. Ask the complainers when they thought they should learn how to do these things. I always say to my kids, "Well, if you really want your sweet, dear old mother following you around in your apartment and at your job, I could certainly do that. Of course, you would look like a dork, but if that's what you want, that's certainly an option." That's usually the end of that.

It is interesting that when you explain to your children the *why* of things, you can get tremendous buy-in. Before this, your kids probably looked upon chores as strictly torture inflicted upon them by lazy parents and didn't understand that they were a means to an end. Having them actually see and understand all the things they need to know how to do to be adults will also get them a little bit intrigued and excited.

Now, if your children are teenagers, it will be interesting to go through this list and cross off the things they already know how to do. They might actually be rather surprised at how much they've already learned. You can then identify those things that are left for them to learn before they reach that magical age of eighteen and independence.

Sometimes kids will say, "This is so stupid. Why do I have to learn how to iron? I can just hire someone to do that." I love hearing that one from my kids. I just smile and say, "Yes, you could hire someone. But until you're independently wealthy, you may want to know how to do it yourself." It's also a good idea to have teens fill in things *they* want to learn before they leave home. Some teens will get really excited about it all and understand The Plan. Some will dig in their heels and resist any participation whatsoever. Hang in there. We'll be sharing some tips for dealing with that later on.

Throughout this experience, keep the family focused on the end goal. Every child can agree on that one—they want to be independent, and the sooner the better.

Training

Have a separate list for each child that you keep on your computer or in paper form that you can all refer to. And remember, this is a *training program,* not just chores, not just isolated tasks. This is an overall plan to train your children to be independent adults. Never forget that.

Let's review some strategies for how to train your children.

1. Introduce the child to the task FAR in advance.

For example, you can say, "Matthew, you get to learn how to make salads this year. Isn't that exciting! I think we'll work on that in about three months, so in June, we'll begin." This does a couple of things. The first is that you can gauge the child's reaction. Matthew may be absolutely ecstatic and want to start immediately. Or Matthew may absolutely hate salads and hates the thought of making them even more. Knowing this will help you strategize as to how to go about the training.

Some children will be excited and happy to learn just about everything on the list. Some will like a few things but not others, depending on where their interests are. And then you will have those treasured ones who fight you tooth and nail on everything you try to teach them. Patience and firmness are needed with those children, and yes, I have one of them so I know what you're going through. For those who are negative about it, drop the subject and don't get into a big argument over it. It's enough at this point to bring it up.

The second good thing about introducing the task well in advance is that you can have an observational training period. Man, didn't that sound fancy? That means they can watch you do the job. As you're making the salad for dinner, you can say, "Matthew, can you get me the celery for this salad? I'm making a green salad, so what else should we put in it?" Matthew can then watch you or whoever is cooking over a period of a few months so that by the time it is his turn to do it, he's already learned pretty much how and what to do. That also helps because you have *no* expectations of Matthew during this time; he can watch you without any stress about actually having to do it right then.

2. Select the trainer.

Before you begin the actual training, choose who will do the training. Pay attention here: I said, *choose who will do the training*. In other words, it doesn't always have to be you. I can still remember clearly the Saturday morning when I had finished vacuuming and my dad came over and said, "Merrilee, let me show you how to wind the cord to the vacuum so it doesn't twist or fall off." He then carefully showed me how to do it, explaining how nifty it was and that it now wouldn't twist around or fall off the vacuum easily. Do you know, I am forty-seven years old, and to this day I think of my dad every single time I wind up the vacuum cord. Part of what was so meaningful was that it was my *dad* and not my mom teaching me.

Be creative here. Frankly, some of the best training goes on in sessions with non-parental units. Who can teach your child how to take care of a bicycle? One day my son's bike had a flat and I was busy and my hubby was out of town. I said, "Go over and ask Ernie next door to help you." So off went Parker with his bike and Tanner following along to watch. And dear Ernie got out his tools and spent several hours teaching my boys how to care for their bicycles. They didn't forget what he said, and he had a wonderful time and grew closer to the boys as well. Many times I heard my boys say, "Ernie says you're supposed to do it this way." Think about having Grandma teach your children how to make pies or Auntie Sophie showing them how to sew.

This strategy becomes absolutely crucial when dealing with teenagers (especially the grumpy ones). Sometimes you have to use "stealth training." Many is the time I've gone to a teacher in school or an adult leader in Scouts or church and said, "My son needs to learn how to change a tire on a car. Can you have a class on that so he learns how?" They were only too delighted to have ideas, and my son got trained in the process.

And don't feel that you are imposing. How wonderful would you feel if someone came to you and said, "Merrilee, you have such a wonderful reputation as a bread maker, could you teach my daughter how to do that?" I would first ask if they were taking hallucinogens, but then I would be so flattered! And wouldn't you? You can tap into a wide variety of people through the neighborhood, school, church, Scouts, and so on. Of course, make sure that your chosen trainer is someone you know very well and that your kids aren't totally alone with that person. But a "class" of this sort can be an amazing experience for your children that they will never forget. They never tire of having adults pay attention to them and think that they are important.

There is no tool quite so wonderful for blasting through stereotypes as having a woman teach "guy" things and a man teach "chick" things. Who taught my boys how to make chocolate chip cookies? Their dad. I can still remember the Father's Day cards that year that said, "I love my dad because he helps me bake cookies." The Mother's Day card said something about hiking. I'm sure the kids' teachers were wondering what was going on in our house. My boys were dying to learn how to sew because their male teenage cousin was making skater pants for all his buddies in high school and pulling in a tidy sum. And have Mom teach them about car care, and on it goes. Rarely do we hear, "That's women's work!" when Dad or Grandpa is the one doing the teaching!

Finally, one of the absolute best trainers is the older sibling. This doesn't always work well for the sibling directly next in line, because they're often in conflict. But it works great if you skip a child. For example, my third son needed to learn how to clean the bathroom (always a day of celebration for me). I said to my oldest boy, "Connor, you are so great at cleaning bathrooms; you're practically an expert! Would you train Parker very carefully so that he can do it as well as you?" Of course, his chest puffed up, and my third boy was ecstatic that his older brother was going to pay attention to him.

I had one of the best times of my life listening outside the door to this instruction session. "Now, Parker, you have to clean the toilet like this. You try it. Pretty good, but be sure and get that spot there. Then you have to clean the floor because we have four boys using this bathroom and their aim isn't too hot. I know, it's gross, but we have to do it or it'll get really gross. Now you need to aim better from now on or you'll end up cleaning it up, right?" And on it went until Parker knew how to do it. We affectionately call the boys' bathroom "The Bus Depot," as you can well imagine. But honestly, they keep it pretty clean because they know they'll be the ones cleaning it up.

Using older siblings as trainers can be really effective. It reinforces the training for the older child, and the younger sibling pays close attention. She won't gripe nearly as much because it's not Mom or Dad "making" her do it.

3. Hold several training sessions.

After selecting the trainer, have several training sessions. Did you know that it takes an average child seven or eight presentations to learn something? So when you're having your training sessions, you need to repeat them many, many times until the child understands the procedure thoroughly. While you're training, be very specific. Don't just say, "Okay, clean your bedroom." That is meaningless. The children will put everything on top of the bed and say, "Voila! The room is clean!" Okay, maybe they won't say "voila," but they will insist that the bedroom is clean. Or they'll cram everything under their bed or in their closet and say, "There—all done!"

So we must be specific. I often made up 3-by-5 cards with detailed steps listed. For example, cleaning the bedroom may have the following steps:

1. Make your bed.
2. Take everything off your dresser that doesn't belong there and close all the drawers.
3. Put all your toys in the toy box.
4. Pick up everything off the floor and put it where it belongs.
5. Check your closet floor so that nothing is left but the hamper and your shoes.

Then you go through each step with the child so you can be sure he understands it. Stop after each step and ask, "Do you have any questions on how to do this or what this means?" I repeat, be very, very specific.

Finally, be nonjudgmental. Tell your children that these are training sessions so that they can learn how to do the task, just like the famous sports stars have training camps. If they mess up, just say, "Oh, Alex, when we make the bed, we put the pillow here. Can you practice that part?" Be very clear and don't criticize their imperfect efforts. Remember, they need eight presentations to learn how. So don't stop at demonstration number one or two and say, "Didn't I tell you to put the oil cap here?" Just be clear and repeat the instruction, "Honey, when we pull off the oil cap, we set it over here and not on the engine because it can fall in and we'll have a tough time getting it out."

Do *not* lavish on the praise. I know most of us are trained as parents, wanting to promote good self-esteem, to pour on gooey praise until our kids are smothered in it. This is the parent who, when the child makes the bed for the first time and it looks pretty bad, will jump up and down clapping and smiling, "Yippee! Sarah made the bed. What a *wonderful* job, Sarah. You're so smart and so great and so wonderful!" Pretty soon Mom has dragged in the whole family and they're all beaming and jumping up and down and praising Sarah on the mediocre bed-making job on her first attempt and they're calling the grandmas and grandpas and on and on it goes. Resist the Praise Overkill Syndrome. Your child is not stupid. She knows that that bed-making job wasn't as good as yours.

The Praise Overkill Syndrome has two effects. First, it

discourages children because they're pretty smart and they know they're not always fabulous. They learn that they can't trust your judgment because you go bonkers over every little thing they do. And so they do not get a good perception of when they're really doing well. They end up with lower self-esteem—the opposite of what the parent was shooting for. Second, they get really lazy. They figure, "Hey, I can do a lousy job and Mom's going to go bananas." You can spot teenagers who have parents suffering from this syndrome a mile away. They are lazy and unmotivated and extremely self-absorbed. And why shouldn't they be? Mom and Dad have trained them to be that way because they end up dripping on praise and applause for the slightest effort.

So put a lid on it. A simple statement, "That was a good effort for your first time," or "Good job," will do.

Don't insist on perfection for a long time. Just keep training. And when the kids mess up, you can reassure them, "We're just in the training period. You're *supposed* to mess up. That's called learning. Don't worry. You'll get the hang of it after you practice."

Mostly you as a parent need to remember that these are training sessions. Your job is to provide clear training on the various aspects of the task and to have *the child* performing the task and learning how.

4. Follow up with practice sessions.

After many training sessions, allow the children to have some practice sessions. Have them perform the task and then let you check it. Make the checking fairly positive. If they do it incorrectly, you can say, "Oh, maybe you didn't understand this clearly when we were training. Let's practice this." Have them do it over and over if the task lends itself to that. Be quite open about things, "Ashley, these are practice sessions where we can see if you've learned how to do this, so just do your best and ask questions if you have problems with it."

Often, it helps to have these "practice sessions" become chores. Say, for example, you've taught your daughter how to weed the flower beds. You can then have that job assigned as her chore for three months so that she can have lots of opportunities to practice. Be sure to check afterward to see if more teaching needs to occur. Note that I said "teaching," not yelling, criticizing, or berating.

In fact, the idea of "teaching" is a wonderful tool that I use quite often. Suppose my teenager does a lousy job at weeding. Now, he's been doing this for about ten years, but I'll say, "Gee, honey, perhaps I need to teach you again a little better. Let's have a training session so I can show you that you actually have to pull the *roots* out when you're weeding and throw the pulled weeds into the garbage can." He will roll his eyes and say, "*Mom,* I already *know* that." I respond, "Oh, gee, from the looks of this flower bed it didn't look like you did. Well, why don't you go practice it a bit more." That goes over a lot better than, "Get out there and pull all the weeds like you were told, you dumb-head!" Although I know it is tempting to lose your temper, and I'm sure I have done so many times, you can rely on this "training" mind-set to get the same result in a more positive—or at least humorous—way.

If your child is consistently doing a poor job, stop and pull it off his or her chore list and go back to training sessions. Now, I don't want you to think these "sessions" need to be long, drawn-out affairs. Sometimes they're two minutes. "Okay, here's how you use a pay phone." Boom. Two minutes. "Now you try it." Bingo. About one or two times and you're done. Much of the training will be this simple. Then, having many of these tasks incorporated into chores really reinforces the training and allows lots of practice.

5. Incorporate the task into your lifestyle.

Eventually the children will master the tasks you've been training them to do. When that happens, step back and let them incorporate those things into their lifestyle. When your child learns how to make his own doctor's appointments, for instance, stand back. Hand him the phone and say, "Here, honey, you need a physical for camp. Make the doctor's appointment," and let him have at it.

The general rule: If they can do it, don't do it for them. If they can tell the stylist how they want their hair cut, keep your mouth shut and let them. I love it when the barber says to me, "Mom, how would you like his hair cut?" I respond, "It's his head, ask him." And then I sit down with a magazine and bury my head in it and listen as my young son responds, "I'll have a short boy's haircut with a #2 trimmer around the edges, block the nape, and no sideburns." The stylist smiles and says, "Okay, let's go." Last month, an older guy sitting in the chair next to one of my sons said, "Gee, I don't even know what size trimmer they use on my head." I just smiled as my son beamed.

If they can make their snacks, let them. If they can pick out their clothes, let them. I can remember one time I was giving a lecture on this topic, and a woman in the audience told me that her sister was still picking out her husband's clothes. We all gasped in shock thinking there was no way that could be true. She said, "Oh, yes. His mother always laid out his clothes, and he told his wife that was *her* job. She's been doing it for over twenty years!" That's certainly an extreme example, but shouldn't she get a clue that he's fully capable of doing this himself?

In fact, I'll share with you a little tip. At the beginning of the school year, I tell my children's teachers: "In our home we try to teach and foster independence in our children. So our kids pick out their own clothing and, depending on the age, may be washing their own clothes. I hope you will be supportive of this." That way if my kids go to school looking like refugees, the teacher will nod her head and say, "Isn't that wonderful! Little Joey obviously picked out those clothes all by himself. What wonderful parents he has to teach him to be independent!" Ha! No guilty feelings whatsoever.

As your children acquire these skills and master them, let them go and make them part of their own lives. This can sometimes be difficult to do. But resist the urge to slow your kids down.

You are probably wondering how far to take this. Frankly, at this point my kids can do so much I could just sit around and do nothing for them. Remember to keep things in balance. For example, my kids can wash their own clothes, and during the summer when they have more time, they do just that. During the school year, they bring their clothes down and I run them through the cycles, and then they pick up the baskets full of clean clothes and take them back up in their rooms to put away. They're hanging on to the skills, and we've adapted the requirements to fit their time constraints. Also, it's fine to keep doing a few things (note I said a *few*) that you do as part of your nurturing.

Hilda had taught all her children to cook. But every morning, she made them breakfast as an expression of her love and nurture. Roger knew his kids were capable of doing the dishes, but he would always do them on Sunday after the big family dinner. This was his expression of nurture with the family. Each of us will have things we hang on to and use to express our love and caring. Just make sure that your kids know how to do these jobs (remember the Daddy Oil Fairy?) and check to be certain that you don't have your nurture in overdrive.

Implementation Tips

Now that we've reviewed the basics of The Plan, let's review some tips on how to implement it.

1. Start at the beginning of summer or at the beginning of the calendar year.

Starting at the beginning of the school year is about the worst time because your kids are in high-stress mode. Exception: If your children are all small, September can be a good time, and you can call this program "Grown-up School" or something fun to fake them out.

Summer is really an ideal time because by day #2 your kids are bored out of their gourds and looking for something to do. We refer to it as "Training Time," and they actually get excited about it.

2. Decide on a timetable and write it into the family calendar.

Write down "John—sew on buttons" or "Maria—paint house" on the date you're going to work on teaching this skill. If they're older, have them write the tasks on *their* calendars as well. Write down the training sessions so that you treat them with seriousness.

3. Vary who does the training.

Remember that The Plan works better if the trainer isn't always Mom or Dad. So if Dad did the last training, put in Grandma or Cousin Louie or the neighbor—mix it up whenever possible. The kids will like the variety and are less likely to get bored or lippy.

4. Vary the tracking methods.

Remember that kids love variety. So sometimes you might track their progress on the computer. Sometimes post the list on the fridge. Sometimes keep it in your Palm (or on theirs!). Use a variety of methods. Use stickers, use cards, use a visual thermo-meter. Try all different ways.

5. Tie the passing off of training items to privileges.

Of all the tips, *this* is the most important. Tying training to privileges is the surest way to get your teenagers or belligerent ones to actually participate.

Your child wants to start baby-sitting? That's great. But you tell them that in order to have the skills and maturity necessary to begin making the big bucks from poor, trapped parents, they first have to master some skills. To be able to baby-sit, they need to pass off basic first aid, make phone calls, know how to con-tact authorities, do CPR, take a baby-sitting class, and fix simple meals. They will be highly motivated. We usually start this chain of skills a year before they want to baby-sit and hold that out as the carrot. The kids can actually use this in advertising to par-ents. Wouldn't you want a sitter who knew how to do all those things?

Your teenager wants to drive the car? Fantastic! This is absolutely primo training opportunity. You sit down with them and review the list and say, "Well, to drive the car you need to know the following: pumping gas, changing a flat, simple main-tenance, getting insurance, how to buy a car, finances, checking account," and so on. They'll try to negotiate. "Why do I have to know how to buy a car?" You answer, "So that you will value what you are driving." You may have to simulate some of the training if your family isn't actually purchasing a car. Take the child to the dealer and pretend you are. Sometimes I talk to the salesman in advance and then step back and let them have at it. Tremendous learning opportunity. The more important the priv-ilege is to the child, the more you can get away with requiring the training to be passed off. Just walk the tightrope; don't push this so far that they give up altogether.

This also works well for younger children. They want to spend the night at a friend's house? They need to be able to make the bed, make phone calls, and care for their own hygiene needs. They want to get a new bike? Work on tithing, having a little job, and fixing bikes in general.

Tying the training to privileges is a great way to get your kids to really participate. It also serves another valuable purpose—it ties the whole plan together. Now the children aren't looking at chores and training in isolation. They see how The Plan all fits together. They begin to understand that this set of skills leads to the more adult skill. And it gives them tremendous maturity that will help out when they do acquire that adult skill. How many teens do you know who, as a matter of course, just go out and get their driver's license when they're sixteen, without having acquired the financial or mechanical skills we've discussed? Or worse yet, Mom and Dad give them a car! (Are they nuts?) How responsible and careful will those kids be? If they actually have to pay for their insurance, buy their own gas, learn how to care for a car, and understand that peeling out chews up tires that they will have to help replace, they will be much more responsible and mature. Who would you rather have driving *your* car, or, even more important, driving around your other children?

6. Use rewards!

Do I believe in bribery? You bet! But dangle the carrot out there and don't give it to them in advance. That never works, regardless of how many extremely articulate teenagers are arguing vociferously for it. "If you let me go to that party this weekend, I *promise* I'll sit down and review mutual funds with you." Yeah, right.

Rewards are a great way to get children to participate in The Plan. This is why summer is an especially nice time to work on it. In our family, we would identify all the things they needed to

45

learn and then set up a point system: going to the movies when you pass off five, an ice cream for three, or even a trip to Disneyland for so many accumulated family points. They would work like little Trojans to get the rewards, and it was fun family time.

Just make sure to choose rewards that appeal to your child or they won't work. *You* may think that going to Disneyland with the whole family would be just wonderful. Your twelve-year-old daughter may consider it absolute torture. So ask the kids, "What kind of reward would you like?" You may be surprised. Often, their desired rewards are easier or cheaper than what you would have suggested.

Remember—*kids want to be taken seriously.* They want to be treated like adults as soon as possible. They want their lives and their abilities to be respected. So treat this like it is, a serious plan for them to get where they want to be and to become who they want to be.

Now, let's be realistic, in the short run, implementing The Plan is harder and more work for Mom and Dad. You may be absolutely exhausted right now just having read about it. Don't worry.

Just keep that end goal in mind.

In the long run, this plan is much easier and far better for your child. You can chuck this all and just go along day to day hoping vaguely that your children will pick up everything they need to know. You can hang in there until they turn eighteen, and then change the locks.

Or you can make a commitment to train your children to be independent. What gift would you like to give your children? Only you can decide and make the long-term commitment necessary to pull it all off.

"Self-sufficiency is the yardstick of self-esteem. The road to self-sufficiency is paved with frustration, disappointment, failure, falling flat on one's face, and other equally 'unhappy' experiences. We cannot afford to deny children these things," advises John Rosemond (*Daily Guide to Parenting,* Nov. 27).

But let me share with you the end results. You will have children who can take care of their bedrooms, take care of their clothes, handle the car, handle their money, prepare food, and talk to you intelligently about a variety of topics. It is incredible. You will have children who are mature and experienced. You will have children who ooze self-confidence because they know they can handle adult things. You will have children who don't run to you every two seconds with, "Mommy, Mommy! Can you do this?" or "Mom, I have to have this done right now!" You will have children who say, "Dad, what do you think about the new tax bill?" It's kind of weird, I know. But in a good way.

You will have children who exhibit independence early and often. You will have the mental space and the energy to work on transferring those values and beliefs that are so important to you. You will have a home that hums a lot. It won't always be perfect, and your kids will mess up sometimes. But that's their job.

Your job is to train them.

CHAPTER 4

Getting Kids to Work: Chores and Beyond

Picture this—it's Saturday morning. Your children all bounce out of their beds, make them neatly, say their prayers, wash their faces, brush their teeth, and come bounding out to greet you for the day. They rush to the kitchen to see what chores they get to do that day. Squeals of delight pierce the air as they rush about the home doing all of their chores until the house shines. They then run up to ask you if there is anything they can do to help . . .

Okay, it's time to snap out of it. Fantasies like that can be dangerous to one's mental health.

To me, the funniest part of the topic of chores and work is the parents. Parents are hilarious. I was speaking to a dad who said that he had really messed up as a parent because his children never volunteered to help around the house. He went on and on, saying that if he had done a better job, he was sure his children would be more helpful. I stopped him right there. "What planet are you from!?" I quizzed him. He looked at me, shocked.

"When you were young, did you *ever* go up to your parents and volunteer to help?" I asked.

"Well, no," he admitted reluctantly.

"And did you have good parents?" I asked.

"Oh, yes," he said, "They were great."

"Do you happen to know *any* children who volunteer willingly to help?" I asked.

"Well, no," he said, "But there probably are some." Well, maybe on Neptune . . .

So let's all wake up to the news flash of the day:

THERE ARE NO FUNCTIONAL CHILDREN ON THE PLANET WHO WILLINGLY RUN TO THEIR PARENTS AND ASK IF THEY CAN HELP.

I'm sure there are one or two abnormal kids floating around out there, but if you check them out carefully, I'm sure there's some manipulation going on somewhere. It's just not natural.

Another news flash:

KIDS DO NOT LOVE DOING CHORES—NOT EVEN MY KIDS.

Parents ask me all the time, "How do you get your children to do their chores? Mine won't do them like yours do." It cracks me up. Like they think my kids are these little perfect angels who run around working all the time.

There is a certain element to kids' work that I believe is absolutely crucial to the normal development of our children and the normal evolution of the family. That element is: grumbling (known in the scriptures as murmuring). This can escalate to whining, complaining, crying, wailing, howling . . . you get the general picture. If this element does not exist, there is something seriously abnormal going on.

There, now, don't you feel better? Now you know your family is normal.

With all that said, let's talk about how to make "doing chores" an excellent opportunity for growth and training, and about how in the world you can get your kids to work.

49

Develop a Backbone

Using chores as a training method cannot be done by invertebrate parents. I'm sure some amoeba out there will disagree, but by and large, the parents must be firmly in control and have their wits about them or this system will fail.

If you go into the assigning of chores with the attitude that, "These poor children are soooo busy and soooo overworked and they have soooo much to face these days and they have soooo much homework and woe is me, what a burden they have," you might as well give up right then and there because your children will milk that for all it's worth.

As I said, parents are rather funny. They give up trying to get their kids to do chores because getting kids to work is so incredibly hard. Then they moan and groan and wonder why their kids are lazy, self-centered, and largely unmotivated. You *must* have a backbone or your kids will never develop one of their own. There isn't a "Work Fairy" who will come around and just whop your children on the side of the head with a wand and make them instantly love to work. At least, I've never seen one in action—by all means, let me know if you find one.

On the other hand, if you approach the issue of chores with a militant attitude and a total control-freak mind-set, you will also fail miserably because your children will use every trick in the book to defeat you.

So you need to prepare mentally. Keep the end goal in mind. Be firm and clear and unmovable. Be assertive and wonderfully centered. *Now* you're ready.

Remember the Importance of Work

Doesn't it seem these days as if we find ourselves surrounded by work-phobic youth? These kids are largely a result of lazy parents; that is, parents who take the easy road. I know that sounds harsh, but I believe that it is true. Parents have to be the ones who understand the importance of *everyone working* to make up a good family. They understand the end goal. They understand that it'll be hard for quite a while to get their children to take responsibility for their work assignments. But they are willing to stay committed to this goal.

Sometimes, as I look around, I wonder if my children are the only ones who do chores beyond self-maintenance. Self-maintenance tasks are pseudo-chores: "make your bed" or "pick up your toys" or "brush your teeth" or "clean your room." Those aren't chores that contribute to the family; they're just self-maintenance. Any three-year-old can do those things. In fact, it's sort of a running joke in our neighborhood and ward that if someone's children complain, the parents threaten them with, "Keep it up and we'll send you to the Boyacks' where the children really have to work!" This kind of freaks me out because it makes us sound like we're running a child sweatshop over here!

By and large, parents have forgotten how important work is in the home. They have a hard time getting their children to work, so they give up. It's easier to hire maids and gardeners or to do it all themselves.

But I know that you are not a foolish parent who would ever do such a thing. You know the value of having your children work—and work a lot!

Elder Dallin H. Oaks commented on this topic as follows: "Families unite when they do meaningful things together. Children should work together under the leadership of parents. Common employment, even on a part-time basis, is valuable. So is a family garden. Common projects to help others are also desirable. Families may establish a perpetual missionary fund. They can research and write family histories and share them with others. They can organize family reunions. They can educate family members in the basic skills of living, including managing finances, maintaining property, and broadening their general education. The learning of languages is a useful preparation for missionary service and modern life. The teachers of these subjects can be parents or grandparents or other members of the extended family" ("Parental Leadership in the Family," *Ensign,* June 1985, 7).

Making home work a priority is crucial. Note I did not say "homework" but "home work," meaning the work we do around our home to contribute to the family unit. It is fascinating that parents spend incredible amounts of time monitoring school homework but completely ignore crucial work around the home. There have been times when my children have been late to school because they did not finish tasks at home. (And my children are always stunned when I do not excuse those tardies.) One day, my sister Kathe noticed that her daughter had gone off to school and had not made her bed or straightened her room. Kathe hopped in the car and drove off to school. There was her daughter swinging away on the swing set before school was to begin. Kacy saw her mom coming and ducked her head. "You didn't finish your work," said Kathe. And she took Kacy home to finish her work and then took her back to school.

Two weeks later, Kacy had been letting her work slip again and had been warned. That morning, Kathe noted that her daughter was not ready for school. She called the school to notify them that her daughter would not be attending school that day. The school secretary asked the reason for the absence. My sister replied, "My daughter has not finished her chore assignments at home and she will be staying home all day to work." The secretary was pleased. "That's so great," she replied. "I wish more parents would teach their children how to work at home." And so little Kacy stayed home and worked all day . . . and learned the importance of working at home. I'm happy to report, she is now an excellent wife, mom, and homemaker.

I've had both reactions from school. I did this with one of my children and the school secretary said, "Well, that's not considered an excused absence." I replied, "Gee, that's too bad. Then just put it down as unexcused." She condescendingly replied, "Well, that would make the child truant and I might have to report this to the authorities." I chuckled, "Feel free! My most important job is to raise independent children. In order to do that, I think it is crucial to teach them how to work at home. If a law officer wants to discuss my parenting with me, by all means give him a call." She backed down and, of course, did not make the call. But be aware that you can't use this tactic often or it could cause problems. Frankly, it took only once or twice with each child to get the point across.

If you place a serious value on the things your kids learn and do at home, so will they. If you treat those things as the last priority, so will they.

As adults, we work for the rest of our lives—whether we are homemakers or running a company. The training for that work rests largely in learning how to work as a youth. God told Adam, "By the sweat of thy face shalt thou eat bread . . ." (Moses 4:25). Kids don't learn to sweat much playing X-Box all day.

Use "The Plan"

Chores should evolve from The Plan. What I mean is that you should look at what tasks your children are scheduled to be learning and turn those into chores. As I mentioned in the previous chapter, if your child is to learn vacuuming, by all means, assign that as his or her chore for a few months after the training period. If children are to learn weeding, assign that as their chore, and so forth.

When you assign these chores, explain to the children that now that they are learning this task, they get a chance to practice it. Reactions will vary on this, but the idea reinforces The Plan and shows how they're going to learn and progress. You can explain, "Jose, this is your chance to really be trained in doing these things so you can take care of yourself when you're a grown-up."

You can list all the chores that need to be done and then coordinate them with where all your children are on their own individual plans. Get the work done and complete their training at the same time!

Use Lots of Methods

I know you were sitting there waiting for me to give you "The Perfect Chore Chart" that would cure all your motivation problems and turn out perfect children. Oh, please.

Let me ask you this. Do you serve the same meal day after day after day? Do you wear the same clothes day after day after day? Do you go see the same movie week after week after week? Of course not. That would be . . . go ahead and say it . . . *boring*.

Exactly my point. To use the same method of assigning chores all the time is incredibly dull; it's no wonder the kids lose interest. So spice it up! Try new things! Switch it around after a few months. Use one way in the school year and a different one in the summer. If something doesn't work, chuck it and try something else.

Some methods will work at a certain age and won't at a different age. Some will work well with your older kids and bomb completely with the younger ones. It's important that you be flexible and keep trying new ideas and *not feel like you failed*.

My sister, the Fabulous Mother Kathe, had a great method. She had a banner-like personal chore chart hanging in the kids' rooms with pockets across the top and bottom. In the pockets were cards listing the daily chores or assignments. As the child completed these, he or she moved them to the row of pockets for "done" items. This system worked famously for my sister. The house and yard stayed clean, the children were on task, and it was a smashing success.

So when I had my children, I dutifully made them individual chore charts with pockets. And I tried, and I tried, and I tried to make this method work. It bombed out completely. I could not figure out how I had messed it up. Then one day when I was talking to Kathe, I said, "What time did your children have to leave for school?" She replied that they left about 8:45 A.M. "Aha!" I retorted, "that's *it*. My kids leave at 7:00 A.M.!" "Oh, man," she said, "There's no way we could have done our chores like that if my kids left at 7:00." Precisely! So that very week I sat the little lovelies down and reported that we were going to a weekend chore system, and they all shouted with joy.

So if one method does not work, don't give up! Just move on and keep searching and making changes.

Let me talk about a variety of systems for assigning home work. You can pick and choose from these ideas or create your own.

1. Pocket chart. Each child has a chart with two pockets, "to-do" and "done." In the "to-do" pocket are several cards: pray, straighten room, brush teeth, and so on. As the child completes the task, he or she puts the card in the "done" pocket. Each day, my sister would add to each child's "to-do" pocket a couple of small daily chores such as vacuum one room or scrub the sink. This is an excellent system if you have young ones or a late starting time for school. It is effective in creating good daily habits.

2. Zone management. In this system, the house is divided into zones and each person is responsible for keeping his or her zone clean and tidy all the time. Zones rotate monthly. This is a pretty good plan for learning overall cleaning, but it didn't work too well for us because my children became violent when others left items in their zones and they had to clean them up. Okay, not *violent,* maybe, but they sure thought about it intensely.

3. *Chore wheel.* This is a rotating chart listing chores that change every week. This idea is good if the children are of similar abilities, and it adds variety. I didn't like it as well because if a kid did a lousy job the week before, it fell on the next person to pick up the slack. But this can be a fun variation.

4. *Random choice.* With this method, the kids choose their chores each week in a random way. One mom blew up balloons with the chores written inside and had the kids pop them. Another used a dartboard with the chores attached to it; whatever you hit was your chore that week. This could be fun on occasion, but I'm not sure I could live with it on a regular basis; it seems to involve lots of parental maintenance.

5. *Monthly rotation.* We are currently using this system, and it works well for older kids. We rotate the chores monthly, rather than weekly. I found that if the children have to do the same task for the whole month, they're less likely to do a skim-type job because they know they're still the ones having to do it the next week. Plus it gives them time to really learn to do the chore well and builds up skills. It also gives them some of the sense of ownership that is such a part of the "zone management" system, which is good.

For the past few years, we've been using a monthly rotation with A and B weeks. Now, doesn't that sound fancy! This is how it's working: We have A-week chores that are household chores such as vacuuming, sweeping, and cleaning bathrooms. My kids learned all of these at young ages. But then I realized that they needed to learn other kinds of chores as well. So we came up with the B-week chores, which are outside chores like weeding, fertilizing the yard, sweeping the outside, and so on.

So one week the kids do A-week chores, and the next week

they do B-week chores. This adds variety, and it gets both the inside and the outside done. It also gives the children crucial training and experience in lots of chores, not just house stuff.

And each month, they switch to a new set of chores. Refer to the chart on the next page to see how it works. For a couple of years, I would initial when the chore was done. But now they've got the system down pretty smoothly, so I'm generally lazy on the initialing part.

(I know, you're asking who cleans the house on B-week. Very funny, oh curious ones. I feel it is my duty to assist a sweet woman who can clean my house in half a day from top to bottom while it would take me three days with all the phone calls and interruptions! Yes, my two favorite days of the month are when Lupe comes to visit. Love that woman.)

6. *Blitz method.* This is where the whole family pitches in and cleans the whole house or a specific room in one time period. We use this method from time to time, but not terribly often. We have teens, so it's a rare occurrence for the whole family even to be home at the same time! But when we have company coming or some other kind of special need, we set the timer, pick a room, and go! We put on some loud Motown music and let 'er rip, and it's fun.

7. *Sixty-second straighten:* The children all go to their rooms and we count out sixty seconds and see how fast they can clean. It's amazing what they can get done in one minute!

These are just a few ideas; I'm sure you'll come up with many more of your own. Feel free to adapt and change as needed and feel good about it. What a wonderful, flexible parent you are!

Use Creative Methods for Other Parenting Needs

Often parents use very creative methods for chores but neglect other problem areas. Let me share a few additional ideas that can make these potential pitfalls a breeze.

#1		8-Nov	15-Nov	22-Nov	29-Nov	6-Dec
A	B	A	B	A	B	A
Boys' bathroom	Fertilize front					
Shake carpets/sweep floor	Shake carpets/sweep floor					
Vacuum FR & nook carpet	Weed back (right side)					
#2						
Master bath	Weed front yard					
Garbage	Garbage					
Vacuum LR/DR, hall carpet	Clean and sweep patio					
#3						
Downstairs bathroom	Sweep front & sidewalk					
Vacuum ALL upstairs	Fertilize back					
Vacuum stairs Dust up	Weed back (left side)					

	#1	#2	#3		Money Chores
Nov	Brennan	Tanner	Parker	$10	Scrub interior doors
Dec	Parker	Brennan	Tanner	$15	Clean walls
Jan	Tanner	Parker	Brennan	$ 5	Vacuum edges

Setting the Table

We came up with a fast and creative method for getting the table set for meals. Each child has a number, and each number has an assignment: plates, glasses, silverware, and so on.

So when we say, "Set the table!" all the kids run in and it's done in a minute. No arguing. Amazing. The number assignments rotate monthly.

If you have more kids than we do, you can add items or assign items to clear from the table.

Seating Arrangements

Isn't this a familiar fight? "I want to sit by the window!" "Jerry got to sit in the front last time." "I want to sit by Mommy!" Oh yes, this battle could go on for years. So let's nip this one in the bud immediately.

Back to the numbers. Ah, those lovely numbers. If you recall, each month a child has a number. It is used in seating like this:

Dining table: Mom and Dad always sit together in the same place, Dad at the head of the table, Mom to his left. Child #1 sits next to Mom, #2 is next to him, #3 around the corner, and #4 next to Dad. On the first of the month, all the kids rotate. This is also a great way to mix it up at the table and talk to different kids.

Car: Or, I may as well say it, minivan, although you may be one of those people driving around in a behemoth that masquerades as a vehicle. I can't drive anything that looks like it could squash a VW Beetle.

Windows and front seats: we all know that those constitute premium seating. So here's how it works.

The passenger seat next to Mom (who is permanently glued to her driver's seat in the car) is called shotgun. Shotgun is based on months: Each child over the age of twelve is assigned a month at a time to sit there. (For safety reasons, children under twelve do not ever sit in the front seat!) For example, Parker sat shot-gun on the even months and Brennan sat there on the odd months. Odd was an appropriate choice for him! (Just kidding, Brennan.) Because Mom is often in the shotgun seat, such as when the family is going to church or on an outing, the rotation of that place is a bit different from the rest of the premium spots.

In the next row of seats in our car, Seat #1 is directly behind the driver. Seat #2 is behind shotgun. In the back row of seats, Seat #3 is behind #2 and #4 is behind #1. So they rotate in a circle. Got it? Actually, it doesn't matter how you number the seats, just assign the numbers and go from there.

Seating assignments rotate monthly and are *strictly* adhered to. We've even been known to leave children at home because they would not sit where they were supposed to.

And the numbers go further:

Sunday Showers

Always thrilling to get the entire family showered and dressed and ready for church, right? Voila! Solution! Child #1 has to shower first, #2 next, and so forth. No more arguing over who has to start. Of course, this is in a household with all males. Perhaps in your home you have girls who fight over who gets to get in the shower first. Oh, what joy! I can't image how awesome that must be! And you thought it was a problem . . . oh, pish-tosh. Count your lucky stars that they want to clean themselves without coercion. If that's the case at your house, you could use this in reverse: #1 *gets* to get in the shower first. Oh, man, I can't even picture that. Heaven!

The numbering system is eminently fair, provides monthly variety, and is a piece of cake to keep track of. The kids now keep track of who is assigned what number, so they pretty much enforce things themselves.

Dishwasher

Emptying the dreaded dishwasher is also one of those bicker points in a family. We simply have a daily schedule:

Sunday—Brennan

Monday—Brennan

Tuesday—Parker

Wednesday—Parker

Thursday—Tanner

Friday—Tanner

Saturday—Mom (I hate that! I try to use paper products on Saturdays.)

If the dishwasher finishes cleaning on their day, then they empty it. If they are slow, and dirty dishes start piling up, well, lucky for them! They get to empty the dishwasher *and* load any dirty dishes that have accumulated around the kitchen. If the dishwasher is not run on one of their days, they're off the hook.

You will note that Daddy Steve is not on the list. That's because he is usually the Dinner Cleanup Coordinator. The rule in our home is whoever cooks does not have to clean up. If I

61

cook dinner, Dad supervises cleanup. If he cooks, I supervise cleanup. Every child clears his own dishes and three other items: snap, snap, and it's done. When I was a kid, I always dreaded being stuck with dishes and having the whole family leave, so we've done it differently. It's very fast and we all work together, which I like much better.

Dog Care

Caring for the family dog (or cat or pig or whatever) is another area crying out for a schedule. I'm always disappointed with parents who buy a family pet and then allow themselves to get stuck with all the pet care. None of that!

We use the same schedule for taking care of the dog as we do for the dishwasher. So each child would have a day or two where he was responsible for letting the dog out in the morning, feeding her, and putting her in at night. This has changed over time. Right now we have only one child who is not attending early morning seminary, so he usually lets the dog out in the morning and feeds her, and the other two take turns putting her in.

Daddy is in charge of walking the dog daily. Maggie exercises her master quite well. They average about 850 miles per year!

Whenever you have an area that's causing contention in the home, try looking at it from a problem-solving viewpoint. You can usually come up with a method that can solve it in a fair, reliable, and consistent fashion. Quit fighting the same battles over and over and over. Just take a moment and try a method. And don't be afraid to change or adjust the method until you find one that fits.

It is amazing how many fights you can eliminate if you have a framework in which the kids can function. As you go about solving all those hot points, the family life begins to flow much more easily. Kids are sticklers for fairness, and once they are satisfied that their need for justice is being met, they are usually quite cooperative. If they don't like your system, ask them what method they would use. You might be surprised at their suggestions!

It's critical that children have daily responsibility. It's also very important that they have regular work assignments. Remember the end goal and you will see that work in the home is crucial to help them be prepared to have and run a home of their own. Don't deprive them of that training!

Implementation Tips

None of the methods listed in this chapter will work flawlessly in each and every case. Remember that children are imperfect beings and so are you. Remember that they are, after all, *children,* and by definition haven't mastered themselves or their attitudes. So all of this is a work in progress.

Given that, here are some ideas on implementing chore assignments and other training methods.

Define the chore clearly

Nothing will drive your children more crazy than for you to say, "Go clean the bathroom," if they have no idea what your expectations are until you descend upon them in a crazy rant, screaming, "That's not clean! The mirrors are a mess." For many years, we had 3-by-5 cards for each chore defining clearly what was involved in doing that chore so there were no questions.

Set a definite time frame

Presenting a vague timeline ("get your chores done on Saturday") is setting up yourself for defeat. Pick a definite time, such as, "This list of chores must be done by 12 noon on Saturday," and have consequences that can be evoked if the jobs are not completed, such as a loss of privileges or, my personal favorite, "penalty chores." Mopping was always my favorite penalty chore to impose because I hated doing it myself. But now those disposable, squirting mop heads have changed everything. The kids *love* to mop the floor. Oh well, I still don't like it.

At our house, we say, "Chores must be done before Elvis leaves the building." This simply means that the older kids can't go out with friends or for activities unless their chores are done. Great motivation! For younger children, it can be "chores before cartoons," which also seems to work well.

Have a no-nonsense attitude

Often parents cave in, give second chances, negotiate their advantages away, and otherwise succumb to the mind-numbing whining and complaining from their children. Don't go down that slippery slope! Go into your bedroom and give yourself a pep talk: "I'm raising independent adults here. This is crucial to their development. I can be tough. This is important." Hop around the room a bit, throw those shoulders back, and go back out there and be *firm*.

Use rewards

This is always a contentious point with parents. We do not believe in paying for chores. However, that does not mean that there are no rewards. For little ones, stickers are absolutely fabulous. They *love* stickers. We had big boxes of a huge variety and let our kids pick out what stickers they wanted to put on their charts and which ones they wanted to wear when they were done.

When the kids were little and had finished their daily chores, I would put on red lipstick and give them a big kiss on their foreheads. They would wear their "kiss-mark" all day like a badge of love. Store clerks always got a bang out of it. My boys would proudly say, "My mama loves me!" Sadly, now when I kiss them they look at me with horror and hurriedly wipe off the offending area as they ask, "Did you have *lipstick* on?" But they still love kisses, even if they protest, and I still give them a ton of kisses.

Little children are fairly easy to reward. You can use stickers, magnetic systems, initials, smiley faces, and so on. We would occasionally give rewards for attitude or promptness—if they did their chores willingly or got them all done on time, *sometimes* they would get a coupon for ice cream or something. In such cases, random rewarding works best. Do not give a reward all the time. But if every once in a while you can reward some less-tangible aspect like quality or mood, that will help improve the overall work.

As kids get older, make the rewards fewer and farther between. You want the children to get to the point by about age ten where they just do their chores because we all do them, and that's the expectation. You want to eliminate the mentality that they have to get some tangible reward for everything they do.

Posting Mom's own chore list

I love the "You-are-*so*-lazy!" routine my kids try to pull. Sometimes they try to act as if I am personally punishing them because I don't want to do any work myself. Whatever. So occasionally I freak them out by posting a humungous to-do list of my own chores and asking if they want to trade. That usually nips that in the bud.

Use both arms

If you're married, get your spouse to back you up completely on chores. Often children will respond to instructions from Daddy more readily than from Mommy, so if you're Dad, step up to the plate and supervise! Or you can trade off being in charge. But if one parent is a softy, good luck. Won't work well. Remember to keep discussing the end goal: "Dear, do you want these children to live with us forever—as in, being stuck in this house for their entire mortal existence?"

Be persistent

Day after day, week after week, month after month, just keep plugging away at it. Some weeks will go great; others will be horrendous. Keep working at it. It will get better and easier. But it will never be perfect.

I always crack up when one of my kids says, "You didn't tell me I had to do chores before I could leave!" with all the indignant attitude he can muster. And I chuckle. "How long have you lived in this house? You've been doing chores for fourteen years and now it's a big surprise to you? That's so tragically sad!" I'm not buying it, but they keep trying it. They are persistent, I'll give them that!

There comes an incredible day in all of this when you get payback. A weekend will hit when they will all go do their chores well without a hitch. And you sit back, stunned, and ask, "Were all the planets aligned or something?" Or you realize that you've been swamped for a week and yet the whole house kept humming along without you. And you're rather surprised by how it all flowed. Or your child goes off to college or a mission and writes one of those much longed-for and anticipated letters: "Dear Mom and Dad, I just want to say thank you for all the things you taught me. Thank you for everything you did for me that I didn't appreciate. You did a great job training me." Man, you frame those!

Then you'll realize—it worked! And it was worth it.

CHAPTER 5

Exposing the "ATM Makes Money" Myth

My parents were very private about money. In fact, my discussions with others have led me to believe that such reticence was the norm for their generation. You just didn't talk to your kids about money matters at home. I can understand that: You don't want little Sally going to school the next day saying, "Guess what! My daddy just got a big cut in pay and now he's only making $49,000 a year." Lovely. We all have nightmares about that one.

But keeping our children in the dark about money issues is not the answer. Why is it important to teach children about money? Because they will spend the rest of their lives worrying about it! Knowledge and preparation and experience can eliminate many of the problems they could encounter down the road. That preparation could save their marriage! Think about that. Money is the number-one cause of divorce, and yet we spend very little time preparing our children to handle their finances.

This is a primary area where adult children struggle to be independent. Many have not been taught the basics and have little or no experience in how to handle money, jobs, and so on. Most of us would acknowledge that we didn't know nearly enough when we moved out of our parents' homes, but we don't do much to equip our children any better.

There are obviously privacy issues involved with money. We don't want children running amok with information on our credit card balance, our income, and whether Mom paid the bills on time this month. And yet we can go overboard in protecting that privacy by not discussing crucial principles that our children need to know and understand. I think another big issue here is that many of us also feel uncomfortable with our own understanding of financial issues and so try to avoid the topic as much as possible. But the ostrich approach rarely works well and it is absolutely devastating in raising independent children.

Before we begin teaching our children about financial things, however, it is important that we get a grip on where we are as parents on this issue.

Your Financial Philosophy

It's a good idea to have a discussion with your spouse about your joint philosophy of finances. You may wonder if you even have one. Did you get married and then run from paycheck to paycheck and credit card to credit card? Are you savers or spenders? How do you *feel* about money? How do you *handle* money? These are all excellent things to discuss and try to work out.

You may wonder why this is important to do first, prior to teaching your children. Nothing is quite as confusing as to be taught by a teacher who doesn't really understand the subject. Worse yet is to be taught by two teachers who disagree or who are both clueless. Very unhelpful. If one spouse is going along pushing savings, savings, savings, and the other is sabotaging with messages of spend, spend, spend, you can see how the child will be extremely confused.

Have a Plan for Teaching Kids About Money

You can either put together a plan to teach your children about money or . . . you can plan on hoping that they learn it somewhere else and plan on bailing them out when they run into trouble! Again, I am amazed at parents who never sit down for longer than two seconds to discuss this and wonder why their children rack up credit card debt, bounce checks, and always want to borrow money from them. News flash: There is no "Financial Fairy." *You* are the Financial Fairy!

Parents will often wait until a child has graduated from high school to sit down to talk about money. How ridiculous is that? "So guess what, Son. You need about $50,000 to go to college and about $10,000 for your mission. You're eighteen now. What is your plan?" Guess what? His plan will be to forget college, forget that mission, this is crazy! Even worse are the parents who pay for absolutely everything and then, when the child gets married, say, "Good luck! That's it!" Or horrendously worse are the parents who are still paying off their daughter's credit card after she's been married for five years or slipping their son a few hundred each month. *What are they teaching?*

Now, I know *you* are a fabulous parent. (You're reading this book, aren't you?) And you would never *dream* of doing that. So let's put together a plan for teaching finances to the little bunchkins.

To begin, think back to how you were taught about money. When did your parents start? What went well? What didn't go well? What would you change? I remember being in complete shock about my first utility bill when I left home. I don't know what I was thinking—perhaps I wasn't thinking!—but when it came, I was horrified. I remember my brother being instructed carefully on savings. My dad still talks about it. After all, Brother was saving for a mission. On the other hand, I don't recall my parents having a single conversation with me on how to save, why to save, and what I should save for. So Brother ended up with a tidy nest egg, and I ended up with spender habits that took twenty years to correct. I remember Mom carefully teaching me how to shop and be frugal—she is an absolute master shopper. She can dicker at Sears (and has!). It was a wonderful skill she taught me. I'm sure you could think of many instances of financial training in your own life with your parents.

Here again, it is good to sit down and jot down those things you want your children to learn as well as perhaps some ways of going about teaching those things. Here are some suggestions you can use (or not use) that might help you to begin.

Allowance Issues

So last week I was sitting there in the salon letting my nails dry. (Yes, this is my one extravagance. Well, okay, one of them, anyway.) Across from me were a mother and a young daughter, who had had a full manicure and pedicure paid for by the mother. I was thinking how much money I saved by having sons (not that you would ever catch me paying for those things anyway)! It turned out that the daughter knew me, and we began to chat. We were talking about my son, whom the girl knew, and I mentioned that he was working. The mom was surprised because my son was only fourteen. She said she couldn't get her children to do anything. I said, "Oh, all my children have jobs because they don't get an allowance past age twelve." The girl gasped, as did her mother. I told them that kids get highly motivated to work if they have no income. The mother commented, "I think it was divinely inspired that we were sitting here today." Meanwhile the daughter was shooting visual daggers at me. Sorry, sweetheart. Welcome to independent living.

Allowances are always a tricky issue, fraught with strong

opinions. Lucky for me, I'm writing this, so I get to give you *my* opinion, and you can take it or leave it. Through my lecturing, I've learned that approximately 90 percent of parents give an allowance in some form. I think giving an allowance to young children is the best way to teach tithing and money management. The lessons they learn will be invaluable to them.

At what age is it advisable to begin an allowance? I prefer kindergarten because at that point they are beginning to grasp numbers and values. Before that, they don't have much of a concept. Give one three-year-old a dime and another nine pennies and the one with the dime will cry because he didn't get as much. They just don't understand.

With that said, it is crucial to avoid lavishing stuff on those young children. I feel so sorry for the children I know who have literally hundreds of toys. They are being taught some terrible lessons of greediness, glut, and materialism. Children who are limited to a few toys will be much better off in the long run.

The big issue with allowance is whether to have it be linked to completing chores or not. There are arguments for both sides of the issue. In our family, we do not tie chores and allowance. It takes only one time having your child look up at you and say, "Keep the allowance. I don't want to work," to uncover the flaws in that system. Chores are things we do because we're part of a family. No one pays Mom for cooking (obviously, in my case); no one pays Dad for weeding. There are things we do because our family members all pitch in to do the work that needs to be done for our home and family. To pay the children for everything would give them a very warped sense of reality. Frankly, we do lots of things that no one pays us for, and the earlier they can learn that, the better!

Children may argue with this and call the parents lazy. This will have to be explained many times: "We are all part of a family and we all work. If you don't want to work, you may move to the hotel of your choice, and good luck to you!" I also volunteer the dog's kennel from time to time, as the dog doesn't work much, but they've never found that option terribly appealing.

On the other side of that argument, some parents say, "Yes, but we get paid for our jobs," and they want to teach that message to their children. We solve that as follows: We have regular chores required of every member of the family for which they don't get paid. Then we also have what we call "Money Chores" that the kids can do to earn money.

Money Chores are larger chores requiring extra effort, such as defrosting and cleaning out the freezer, finishing large yard projects, or washing and detailing the car. Those chores provide great opportunities for the kids to earn money while they master those larger, and often rather unappealing, work activities that they really need to learn how to do. We have fairly high standards of excellence for Money Chores, since the kids are getting paid. The minute we let a lousy performance slide by, we're dead in the water. So the rule always is that the Money Chores must be checked and approved by a parent before payment is made. And we talk a lot about what a real job is like and how employers don't pay you in advance.

Money Chores can also be done to earn privileges rather than money. Nothing is quite so wonderful as having your teenage son offer to wash and vacuum the car so he can go to the beach with his friends. Yahoo! This can be a great boon to busy parents. I needed to change the shelf paper in my pantry and kitchen. I offered a per-shelf payment, and gradually, over the course of three months, it got done by the boys. How lovely is that? And how much better than just shelling out five bucks here and there when they whine and beg. When our kids want money, we just say, "Go look at the list of Money Chores and do one."

They value that money so much more than if the Daddy ATM had just spit out a wad of bills.

This system can also really curb the kids' spending. If they know that going to In-N-Out (translation for those of you living in deprived areas: THE best burger place on the planet) will cost them an hour of work, they look at it far differently.

Next, there are allowance timing issues. I must admit that I got a weekly allowance when I was a girl until I began baby-sitting at the age of about twelve. So I thought it was logical to pay a weekly allowance, and I began working that way with my children. In the first few months I almost went bonkers. Who carries around small change and small bills? My hubby and I were constantly scrounging for quarters. It was ridiculous.

You know, sometimes we are truly inspired over silly things. One day my husband and I were talking about how this was driving us crazy, and we both looked at each other and had a dawn of understanding hit us. Okay, well, maybe we were tired and delusional. Anyway, it occurred to us that we didn't *have* to pay a weekly allowance after all. And so we went to a monthly allowance.

On the first Saturday of the month, we would give out allowances to the children. Now, this worked *sooo* well. First of all, it solved our cash dilemma and saved our brains from weekly overload. We could plan on once a month having the appropriate cash amounts. Second, the children got a large amount of cash at one time. This allowed them to buy better stuff. Think about it. You could get $1 a week, and all you could buy would be junk. But with $5 you could buy something a lot more substantial. Of course, we had to put the brakes on their going out and buying pound-sized bags of candy! Third, the children had to manage their money all month. That taught wonderful lessons on frugality and postponing pleasure. They knew that if they spent it all, it was a long time until they got more.

Monthly allowances also helped train them for getting paychecks. Rarely does a job pay every week—most folks get paid either monthly or biweekly. This is wonderful training for the real world in which they will need to budget their money to last.

Now, to another sticky allowance issue—how much? A recent survey done by *Consumer Reports* says that the average allowance for children 9–11 years old is $3 per week with no chores required; kids 11–14 got $5 per week with no chores. In our area, the average child is getting about $40 a month. Incredible, I know. That's about how much *I* get!

Bottom line, don't pay too much. The appropriate amount is an amount that will cause your children to be thrifty and prudent. It is an amount that will teach them the wonderful things they need to know without teaching them negative things you don't want them to learn. So think about them not being able to buy on a whim the latest video game or outfit. Think about them having enough money to have fun but not enough to party every weekend and treat all their friends to the movies. If you aren't sure, err on the side of lower.

Here is our allowance rule: Each child gets $1 per month for each year of his or her age. So a five-year-old gets $5 a month. Plenty. A ten-year-old gets $10. Again, plenty. Now, if that is too strict for you to consider, you could use perhaps $1.50 per year of age, but if you go to $2, I'm going to have to call you for a loan. Again, remember that this dollar amount is enough to help the children learn to manage and enjoy money, but not enough to meet all their needs. You want them to be highly motivated to do Money Chores, remember?

Prepare for the grumbling and complaining to begin. You won't hear much until they're about ten and getting more social. Then they will begin to compare and realize that Joey next door is getting $40 a month for doing absolutely nothing and they're getting $10 and working like Trojans on their chores for free.

Brace yourself. Often, I will commiserate and say, "You poor thing. What suffering you have to endure in this family! How can you stand it?" with a sly smile. Or I will say, "Oh, you have been given such a tremendous gift! Joey will not have such great opportunities to learn how to work and budget his money. He will not learn those values of thrift and prudence that you are learning. You will be such a gifted adult. Aren't you lucky?" Of course, all I get is that look of withering disdain, but I smile nonetheless.

Remember, you want them to *want* to work and earn money. You want them to have to scrimp and save for what they buy. You want them to learn to budget and understand the value of a dollar. Keep reminding yourself of this constantly as they complain. And after a few years or perhaps decades, you'll have it down pat.

It is also important that you have a chat with grandparents and aunts and uncles. Nothing can blow your child's budgeting training faster than a sympathetic grandparent giving them a ton of money. Tell the grandparents to give it to you instead if it will make them feel better.

Tithing

Tithing is an important issue to teach early and well so that by the time the children control all their own money, they have a testimony of it. I so admire converts who are able to embrace this principle, because it's not an easy one. Our children will truly benefit from good training in this area.

The kids found it much easier to pay tithing when they received allowance monthly. Paying a dime a week becomes a little crazy, but paying fifty cents or a dollar a month is much clearer and easier. We set up Fast Sunday, generally the first Sunday of the month, as Tithing Sunday, and everybody filled out their envelopes, had the cash to pay their tithing because they'd just gotten their allowances, and voila! Success!

We discovered that the key to being successful in teaching the children to pay tithing was *our* regularity with it. We paid our own tithing regularly but had to work at helping the children pay theirs regularly. It was difficult to have to orchestrate all the kids' incomes and to have enough cash on hand at the appropriate times. It is tempting to just let it slip by and accumulate, but children truly benefit from regular, monthly payment.

Once I was teaching a Primary class of four- and five-year-olds about tithing. I can remember one particular boy saying, "Is this for real? My dad doesn't do this. I don't think anybody really does this." I got a chuckle out of that because I knew his parents were very faithful and did pay their tithing. He's a deacon now, and his dad's the bishop, and I like to tease him about this a bit. I had the children fill out their envelopes and take their money to the bishop, and we sat and had him talk to them. It made it very real.

You can set up a family home evening along these lines to teach them when they're about that same age, four or five. Again, it is hard for them to understand value, so this is a lesson that needs to be retaught regularly.

Another important part of teaching the principle of tithing is bearing your testimony of it. One day my twelve-year-old came in and sat by my desk and asked me how much tithing I had paid throughout my life so far. It was an intriguing question, so I said, "Let's add it up and see!" I have to say, I was absolutely astounded at the total. (Remember, I'm quite old. . . .) It was enough to buy a house! We both just stared at the total with our jaws slack. I turned to my son and said, "Honey, now you *know* that I know that the Church is true and that this is God's money because there's no way I would give that much money to anyone!" That testimony has stuck with that child to this day.

Bear your testimony of how paying tithing makes you feel. Bear your testimony of what is done with the money. Tell how it is the Lord's money. Reinforce these lessons over and over. Don't just assume the children are picking it up from somewhere during Primary. They need to hear it right from their mom and dad's mouths.

Now, you may hit a snag with this when your children get their first real-live, biweekly-paying jobs. All of a sudden, that $1 a month mushrooms to a much larger amount, and the children are calculating how many CDs they could be buying with that money. The issue of tithing becomes more complicated. Also, at this time they are largely independent and you will not (and should not) *make* them pay their tithing. But try to make it easy on them, especially for the first few months. Get that envelope ready. Offer to cash their check or help them make change to pay their tithing. Encourage them to pay it every time they get a paycheck so it doesn't accumulate to a staggering amount. And bear your testimony a lot. This is, for many people and many teens, a difficult principle. Don't minimize it. They do *not* need to hear, "We've taught you this for a million years. You understand it, so what's your problem?" None of that. It *is* a big deal and a lot more money, and they are in some of their prime spending years, so everything has changed. Patience and love and bearing testimony are key. And remember, they must choose on their own to be obedient. This is not your choice.

Spending

Imagine overhearing this conversation in a store. In fact, you probably *have* heard it—I know I have.

Dad: "You're not going to buy that. That's a ridiculous waste of money."

Son, with his jaw set: "But Dad, this is *my* allowance and I can spend it any way I want to."

Dad: "Oh, no, you don't. That money is mine. I'm not going to let you spend it on that and that's the end of this discussion."

So what has Son been taught? Well, Dad is a control freak, for starters. Son's money is not his own—strings are attached. He can't be trusted to make his own financial decisions. His judgment is lousy. And on and on we could go.

Let's try another take:

Dad #2: "Son, I'm concerned that that toy is poorly made and won't last."

Son #2: "But Dad, this is *my* allowance and I can spend it any way I want to."

Dad #2: "You're right. You make your own decision."

Now Son #2 can buy the toy or he might choose not to. He knows that Dad trusts his judgment and that it is *his* money. He could buy the toy and have it break and learn to look more carefully or to turn to his parents for their opinions. Or he could decide to save his money for something of better quality. Regardless, he is learning spending skills on his own with his parents merely being advisors.

What a marvelous opportunity to learn about value and quality! Your daughter can learn that designer clothes may not be worth the price. Or she might learn that buying something today because her allowance is burning a hole in her pocket may not be the best for her in the long run when she keeps running out of money and her friends want to go to the movies.

Let your children learn these lessons. Nothing teaches better than experience. And when the lesson is a hard one, you don't have to say, "See, I told you so." A more useful statement is, "What did you learn from that?" Be it good or be it bad, they will have learned something, and it's good to reinforce those lessons by talking about them. In summary, then, if you're going to give an allowance, do it with no strings attached on how the money will be spent. You can advise but try to do so in a positive way, without belittling the child's feelings.

It *is* helpful, however, to teach children about having both short-term savings and free spending. You can say, "How much of this do you want for spending immediately and how much do you want to save toward that skateboard you wanted?" This will help them separate their allowance into subcategories rather than going with the perception of "I'll spend whatever is in my pocket." Many a newlywed has to learn this lesson the hard way when the rent and utility bills come and money hasn't been set aside for them.

Also, of course there are a few ground rules about spending in our house—no pound bags of candy unless you want to take over the dental bills. (Nothing curbs candy and soda consumption faster than making your child pay for fillings at the dentist. Works like a charm.) And no items in our home that would drive out the Spirit. I guess that's it. Sometimes the kids have violated these rules, in which case nothing teaches consequences faster than chucking that CD or candy into the garbage can with no reimbursement, preferably under the gooey kitchen garbage on garbage day so it is irretrievable!

Ending Allowance/Adding Clothing Allowance

As important as it is to have an allowance for children, it is equally important to know when to end it. In our home, allowance ends at the age of twelve. We discuss this far in advance so the children are fully aware of it and can be prepared. Why end at twelve? The most important reason is that at this age the children are capable of earning their own money. They are fully able to do enough Money Chores to provide for their spending money, and they can also baby-sit or do yard work for others.

We call this the age of "Financial Accountability." Just as the Lord has taught us that children are accountable at age eight for understanding right and wrong, we feel that they can be financially accountable at age twelve. They understand how to work. They understand how to budget. And it's time to encourage both of those concepts to go into a major practice mode. As I've mentioned, nothing motivates a child more to work than having no money coming in. This also coincides quite nicely, I believe, with the time when their social taste buds are beginning to grow. Clothes and music are becoming important at this age. This is absolutely primo motivation time!

Parents often look at me incredulously when I discuss this. They protest, "But I can't get them to work at all." Of course not. Why should they, when you're supplying their every need and want? If I had someone paying my way, I doubt I would be motivated to work either. Trust me, most of the kids out there will choose to move into action if they know their parents are serious and if the drip-drip from the Mommy and Daddy Magical ATM is cut off.

The second statement I get is, "But they're just children. I think their job is just to do well in school and that's all." The problem with this is that parents who feel this way seem to have a hard time figuring out *when* their children are no longer just children, and meanwhile the kids never learned how to work. I'm not talking about having your child slave away around the neighborhood for hours on end. But almost every child is perfectly capable of having a little baby-sitting job or yard job here and there.

And remember the bottom line, the end goal of independence, always, always, always. You want independent adult children. You want children who are good workers, capable of holding stable jobs. Let's compare approaches:

Mommy and Daddy Indulgent pay their little girl a hefty allowance all the way through school, college, grad school, post-grad school, and the first few years of trying-to-find-a-job-and-find-herself-but-it's-really-expensive-to-live. Gee whiz, they want their daughter to be happy and do well in school. She goes to get her first job. (Now may I insert the recent statement of a friend of mine that his daughter was getting her first full-time job *at the age of 35!* I wanted to scream at him but decided it was inappropriate because we were in the middle of a meeting. Tempting, though . . .) The people interviewing her ask, "Do you have any experience?" She admits she has none. They are somewhat taken aback. "Not even a part-time job?"

"Well, no," she says. "My parents said my job was to do well in school."

"Yes, I see you did pretty well. But you've never worked?"

"No."

Okay, do you think Indulged Princess gets the job? Does she get a good job? Let's give her the benefit of the doubt and say she gets hired. She now has to learn how to work *full-time* and support herself (hopefully) in the process along with everything else she is having to learn.

Compare to Mom and Dad Excellent. (That's you!) At the age of twelve, their daughter begins baby-sitting. She learns to shop carefully and sew a bit to supplement her wardrobe. She grows tired of baby-sitting and decides to learn typing and computer skills. She gets hired at age fourteen to work after school entering computer data. By sixteen she has a part-time job at the local hardware store. At eighteen she gets a full-fledged job for the summer working as a secretary and learns accounting. She works through college and by the time she gets her first, real-live, full-time job, she can take her pick of offers.

I admit it—that was the true story of yours truly. By the time Excellent Daughter (okay, busted—that was me—I had great parents!) goes for her job interviews, she has had six to ten years of work experience. Her resume looks incredible. She makes a lot more money, knows how to work, knows how to keep a job, and on and on.

Focus on the end goal. Sometimes the most important learning our children will do is outside of school. Our kids could get straight A's in school and be clueless on how to hold down a real job.

We'll talk more about children and jobs later in this chapter. But let's first discuss another important milestone reached at that golden age of "Financial Accountability." At age twelve, our kids get a clothing budget. Ah, the golden, coveted clothing budget. It was hilarious as my kids would approach this age—they just couldn't wait to get one. They seemed to forget about the allowance going away. That clothing budget meant they were *like a grown-up!* And we all know how incredibly exciting that idea is to a twelve-year-old.

When the children turn twelve, they get an *annual* clothing and school supplies budget. This is a fixed amount of money determined each year in August. From this amount, they purchase their clothing and school supplies throughout the entire year. They can blow it all in August or spread it out; it is up to them. Let me illustrate with a sample scenario:

Parents and Daughter sit down together and have Daughter write out what clothes and supplies she believes she will need for the year. Need I say it? Be careful here. This is not a bonanza shopping adventure in which Daughter writes down that she needs twelve pairs of shoes. Here again, the key is prudent and thrifty. She is to list *needs,* not wants. They then total this up at Wal-Mart prices. Parents will get much protestation at this stage and rolled eyes and dramatic sighs as Daughter states that she wouldn't be caught dead in Wal-Mart-type clothing. This occurs even with boys, so I am very familiar with the arguments. I tell the children that if they want to buy more expensive clothing, they can feel free to do so—they can either buy fewer clothes or supplement the budget with their own money. Some have supplemented; others grew to love Target and Wal-Mart. Add in school supplies to this budget. Also factor in hand-me-downs. If Daughter needs five dresses and will get two from Older Sister, by all means deduct that.

I'll add a little tip here. I work with a charity called Mothers Without Borders. We do work with international orphans, focusing especially on Africa and India. One of our projects each year is to gather T-shirts and sew T-shirt dresses for the little girls in the orphanages. They literally lined up the little girls last year and had them count how many holes were in their clothes. If they had more than ten holes, they got a new dress. I can hardly talk about this without getting a lump in my throat. This year we sent 600 T-shirts to the boys and 325 dresses to the girls. On my wall in my office I keep two pictures. One is a "before" picture of a large group of Zambian girls in their rags. The second is the same group in their new dresses with beaming smiles.

So . . . before my children and I have this budget conversation, I point to these pictures and say, "Guys, let's keep in perspective how blessed we are. Let's be a bit frugal here so we can send more to these children who really need things." Talk about a course correction! And as we're walking through stores and the kids are agog with potential purchases, I mention it again. "Can you imagine those little Zambian girls here in this store?" Immediate perspective.

So let us continue. Let's say my son gets $250 as a clothing and supplies budget for the year, which starts in August. It starts then because the sales often kick in then for school. That money is all available in August. (If your finances can't handle that, you could pay quarterly, but try for no more often than that.) We have the master list and the clothing budget amount written on a card. Please note that not every child has the same amount. In fact, our fourth son gets a whole lot less because he is the major recipient of hand-me-downs. Yes, yes, life is not fair. Tell that to the orphan girls. (See how well that works? Much better than the starving children in China my mom tried on me because we actually have made and sent these items and we have the children's picture right there in front of us.)

The kids can also get varying amounts because of how fast they grow. I had four boys so nicely spaced that I used to just shift their clothes from one boy's drawer to another. Then Sons #2 and #4 grew faster and suddenly it was more like I had two sets of twins! So growth can be a factor in determining the budget as well. Make no apologies for the differences. That's life. The goal is that they are adequately clothed. That's it.

So they can spend their money all at once if they feel like it, or whatever they choose. Shoes are a big issue. I can remember Connor buying $100 shoes with his first clothing budget and having no money left for a swimsuit, so he had to swim in jeans shorts. He learned quickly (as did his observant brothers). By the time you get to the third or fourth child, they've figured out a lot! They're not quite so picky about the labels anymore. You can certainly say, "Don't forget, you'll need money for shorts in the summer." And remind them. They're still learning. But if they choose to buy anyway, clamp that mouth shut!

Now—a couple of lessons we learned the hard way. Do *not* make church clothes a part of their clothing budget. I learned that when my son grew really fast, had used up most of his budget, and refused to buy church clothes with what little was left. Take that out of the equation so it doesn't become an issue.

Also, talk to them as they're shopping. "Do you think this will go on sale if you wait a few weeks?" "When do you think it's a good time to buy a swimsuit?" Teach them about sales (at the beginning of the season) versus clearance (at the end of the season and a *lot* cheaper). Teach them to shop around and find the same item for less in different stores. It's rather funny: Now my kids educate me. Who knew you could buy shoes so incredibly cheaply on eBay? My kids buy (and sell!) *everything* on eBay and save a bundle.

Ask them, "Do you think that will still fit you in the spring?" Remember, you are teaching all the time, but when working with kids of this age, advising and counseling are better than lecturing. Have them describe to you why they made a particular purchase. It will help them learn to look for value, quality, and price. What wonderful lessons!

Having an annual budget is also a wonderful lesson in itself of spreading things out, keeping track, and planning ahead.

I bless my parents all the time for putting this into place in our family. By the time we were on our own at age eighteen, we had six years' experience! My college roommates had none and had to learn some very painful lessons at a difficult time. By contrast, we knew how to shop, budget, watch sales, plan, do without, learn to sew—I could go on and on!

And let me tell you, kids *love* this. They control a *big* sum of money and can make their own decisions. They know that this is Adult Time and they are ecstatic.

Again, we have one governing rule: Items must be appropriate and modest. Again, you guessed it: Consequences apply! So when Son bought one of those metal-studded belts that looked like he was some giant Doberman pinscher, we warned him he needed to return it as it was not appropriate and detracted from the Spirit in our home. And darn it—he didn't get around to it. Welcome to garbage day—out it went. To this day, he'll occasionally mention, "You know, you owe me $25 for that belt." I just smile. . . .

May I rant for just a moment here? I am raising all sons and so am painfully aware of the impact that immodest clothing on women has on young men. May I really, really urge you parents of young women to have strict rules about clothing? One day I was sitting in the parking lot at the high school on carpool duty with my son and a couple of young men waiting for the last kid to come out. You should have heard the comments as one girl after another walked by. We live in Southern California where the dress standards are appalling. As we watched a fashion parade that looked like it came from a brothel, I said to them, "Do you guys think these outfits are sexy?" The boys said, "Those girls are so skanky. They're disgusting." Interesting. (By the way, translation: *skanky* is like sluttish or trashy.)

Can you imagine how distracting that is to young men? And they're not the only ones. I can still remember the day a quartet of young women stood at the pulpit at church to sing. The girl in front of the bishop had on an incredibly tight short skirt and the poor man was having to look at the wall to avoid staring right at more than he wanted to see.

Please do not allow your daughters to wear immodest clothing. If you can see their belly, tell them to return it or throw it out. If it's too tight, the same. Do not relax the standards. And don't pay for items that go against those standards, I beg of you. If you do, you will teach your daughters that their bodies are to be used for attraction and sexual manipulation. You will teach them that rules are meant to be ignored or bent severely. You will teach them that you believe the prophet is out of touch with reality. You will teach them that you will not require standards to be maintained and that if they wear you down, you will compromise your obedience. Don't do it, even if they rage and rant for years.

Teach your daughter the positives of modest dressing. Have her stand in front of the mirror and ask her if she feels like a daughter of God. Testify to her of what a privilege it is to dress modestly so that you would feel comfortable in His presence. Praise her when she looks beautiful and modest. Praise her for keeping the standards. And teach this principle *early*. Don't wait until age twelve. This starts at about age seven when she first sees movies and TV and all her little friends are ogling the fashions. Okay, thanks so much for letting me rant. I just see parents who cave on this reaping such sadness later on.

Another question on clothing budget: Can the money be used for other things? The only thing we let them transfer this money to is their mission/college savings. *Nothing* else. Otherwise you have a child with the latest Game Boy and one pair of pants. Of course, they use it for school supplies, but that category is narrowly defined. Can it accumulate year to year? Sure, but if that happens, you've probably set the budget too high. Remember, this budget amount changes from year to year and from child to child. Some years the younger ones get more than the older ones, depending on the hand-me-down and growth status. There is no set schedule on this.

Having the clothing budget also takes the edge off of losing the allowance. Somehow the kids don't figure out that if you didn't have this budget, you would have bought them these clothes anyway. Because it's under their total control, they perceive it much differently. Needless to say, it's a big hit and they have no idea all the fantastic lessons they're learning from it along the way.

Job Issues

By now you've figured out that we're pretty much in favor of having children work and have jobs. Let's talk about the elements of jobs and kids.

When should a child work? Money Chores can start as early

as age five—just make them age-appropriate. Again, make them real and valuable. Kids are smart. They know if they're getting away with doing not a whole lot and getting paid too much. By about age eleven, other opportunities begin. The kids can do pet-sitting and house-sitting, which are easy. Have them make a flyer and distribute it through the whole neighborhood. They can walk dogs and do odd jobs.

At age eleven, our kids take a baby-sitting course. No child is allowed to baby-sit in our home until he or she passes that course and understands first aid and basic CPR information. (Usually, we teach our boys using the Boy Scout first aid merit badge book—here again, buy the book and teach the girls as well!) From ages eleven to sixteen, the kids can do a variety of things:

Pet-sitting
House-sitting
Yard work—mowing, weeding, trimming
Housecleaning
Baby-sitting
Walking dogs, children, turtles?
Mother's helper—during parties, rough weeks, and so on
Computer work and typing
Painting
Shoveling snow
Bake sales
Lemonade stands
Helping the elderly or disabled—they can so use just
 a capable pair of helpful hands!
Filing in an office

I could go on and on. The kids get very creative. My nephew sewed skater pants and practically paid his way through high school. I made macramé belts and purses when I was in school, and I chuckle to see that those are back in style now! I used to sell those things like mad. My one son was very computer-savvy and did consulting and Web site design from age thirteen on. Another son loved physical labor and worked for a friend putting in hardwood floors on weekends. He was a big thirteen-year-old and came home happy every Saturday after working with the guys. I know a girl who makes fabulous cinnamon rolls and peddles them around to friends and neighbors.

It is incredible what the kids can come up with. Advertising is key. It is wonderful experience for them to learn to put together a flyer and to contact people. They learn such confidence and verbal skills. Great experiences.

At about age sixteen, the kids want a "real" job. There are numerous opportunities out there. A couple of ground rules apply: We set a minimum standard for grades, and if they slip below that, no work. In every case, their grades have actually improved.

Another rule for us is that there is *no* Sabbath day working. Nothing a teenager does requires breaking the Sabbath. I've seen parents who just shrug their shoulders and say, "Well, they wouldn't hire her unless she worked on Sunday." Okay—so don't take the job. Here again, arm your children in advance. It is interesting when your child goes in boldly and says, "And by the way, I cannot work on Sunday because that violates my religion." When it is phrased in that way, many employers back down. I found it intriguing that there were three Mormon kids working at the store with my son and he was the only one who didn't have to work on Sunday. He was very up front about it and they said okay. Once they scheduled him on Sunday, and he went in and said, "This violates my religious principles. I will not be able to work on Sunday." And they immediately backed down and changed it. But bottom line, any Sunday required, end of job. They don't need this job to feed a family and they need to be firm on that one, as do you.

Should parents get involved in helping kids get jobs? There have been jobs where we got involved and jobs where we didn't. But we waited a long time, until the child was begging for our help. That is key. Do *not* weigh in there at the beginning. Sometimes it's very difficult to get that first real job. If you were looking for a job, you would network with others, wouldn't you? So it's okay for them to network with you. But wait until it is their idea.

Our son Brennan had spent three months applying all over the place to get a job and hadn't gotten hired. It was the middle of an economic slump, and jobs were hard to find. Finally, he said to me, "Mom, I need help getting a job and I really want one at the grocery store." I asked, "Do you really want me to help you?" He said he did, and I said I'd be happy to. I loaded him in the car right that minute (after he changed into handsome clothes), and we drove over to the grocery store up the street. Now, over the past fourteen years I'm sure I've paid for several remodels of this store due to the amount of food consumed by my four sons. Brennan's older brother had worked there for a couple of years. I know the manager very well from my Chamber of Commerce involvement. So in we walked and asked to see the manager.

Tom came walking up and said, "Hi, Merrilee!" I said hello and introduced my son. I said, "This is my son Brennan and he's sixteen."

And Tom said, "I'll take care of it."

I said, "He's a good boy and works very hard. He's been working since he was eleven and he's also a Life Scout."

Tom repeated, "Yup, yup. I'll take care of it. Let me get him an application."

Brennan piped up, "Sir, I have already filled out an application and it's on file."

Tom was impressed. "Okay, I'll have my manager call you

this afternoon to set it up." That's it. Bingo. The kid has a job. As we walked through the store, he was in an absolute daze. Everybody had been trying to get a job there.

But we also had a rather frank discussion. "Son, did you see how fast that was?" I said.

"Yeah, Mom, that was incredible!"

"Yes it was. That is what it means to have a good reputation. I have a reputation in this community for integrity and honesty and hard work. My reputation just got you that job. Now, on this job you not only have to live up to your own reputation but you have to live up to mine. I hope you will respect that, Son."

"Yeah, Mom. Absolutely." He has worked incredibly hard, and they all love him over there. He has been a credit to the family.

So should we as parents get involved? Yes, to a certain point. Helping get them there *when they ask you* can be great. Just don't bail them out if they make mistakes. Don't remind them to get ready to go, orchestrate their schedule, and so on. None of that. This is *their* job. Let them have it. And let them learn from it.

Working for the family or the family business is good experience, but don't limit them to that. Let them go out and get work with others.

Having a boss is such a great experience for a child. Now someone else has high standards that the kid has to uphold. In fact, I've even called the boss and suggested that *he* tell my son to get a haircut. Ha! Works great! And it's not Mom nagging!

Now, a step beyond finding a job is training for a career. You can discuss this informally with your children in their early teenage years. Just point out various jobs and ask them if they're interested. What looks fun about that job? What looks meaningful? Is any part boring? It's good to teach them that every career has boring aspects to it.

Explore further with discussions on preparation. For example, one son had a teachers quorum advisor who was an FBI agent. (Little aside—okay, the Church is true. The advisors for my son's teachers quorum were *huge*. One was an FBI agent who was six-foot-six, and the other was a former professional football player who was about six-foot-five. They picked the boys up for church each week, and my kids knew that if they didn't get out front, Garry would come in and haul them out of bed personally. And he was big enough to do it! It was *fantastic*. We were so sad when those advisors were released, but they called a Border Patrol guy and a cop next. *Love* it.) So Son is now drooling all over a career in the FBI. Imagine his shock when he found out you actually have to have a four-year college degree! Suddenly Son who didn't want to go to college before was now talking about it. Yeah!

Another preparation tactic is as follows: We see people doing horrendously menial work (like holding up a sign on the road for construction workers) and we say, "Gee, no one could make *him* go to college!" Repeat that enough and advanced education becomes very appealing.

Have them take those interest surveys available on the Internet on careers. Have them talk to all kinds of people in all kinds of places. Look at the majors offered at the local university and ask which appeals to them. Talk about what they are looking for in a career. This is *crucial* for daughters. One of the big things they will want is a flexible career that will not impact mothering duties. Have that discussion *before* she decides that being a researcher in the Arctic is looking great. Talk about it in little snippets all the time. And talk with no judgment. When they want to be a professional mountain biker (I'm thinking, What? Is there even such a thing?), ask them, why? Do you think that would work well with being a dad? What would that kind of job mean?

The next step is to guide their jobs to give them a taste of the career path they're interested in. For example, I talked to a mom whose son wants to be a business law attorney. Well, I happen to know one well and offered to set up a job or internship for this kid. Great opportunity! Then he can see—before he goes to college for four years and law school for three—if that's really what he wants. And if that *is* what he wants, his fabulous experience will enrich his education tremendously. Your daughter wants to be a chiropractor? Go to the local one and ask if she can help in the office for a few months. Son wants to have his own business? Set him up with your friend who has one. These jobs can be paid or unpaid, but either way the education will be priceless. Again, this has to be driven by your child—something he or she is interested in, not something *you* want the kid to do.

You would be surprised how many people would be willing to have a young person hang out with them and shadow them. Those who have their own businesses have a lot of control and it's easier to work this out. So use your contacts and your friends and relatives and their contacts to set up these learning experiences. They are priceless. My friend had a son who wanted to be a lawyer. It took about two months of mind-numbing boredom for the boy to realize that a lawyer on TV was nothing like a real lawyer. He changed his mind. Another friend lined up her daughter to be an aide in a teaching environment and the daughter absolutely fell in love with teaching. Great opportunities either way.

Summary

This concludes the first part of our financial training course. We've covered a lot of ground: allowances, tithing, spending, a clothing budget, and job issues. These are the basics. In the next chapter, we'll go a step further and learn how to teach the lifetime financial issues of saving, investing, borrowing, and budgeting.

CHAPTER 6

Financial Training, Part Two: The Advanced Course

Now that your child knows the basics about money, such as where it comes from and where it doesn't, how to earn it and how to spend it, it's time to learn some really exciting things about putting money to work!

Savings Issues

One of the most neglected areas of instruction regarding finances is savings. I daresay if more children were educated on this issue alone, a host of ills from credit problems to bankruptcy to divorce over financial strain would be avoided. In fact, when we taught our children about savings, we greatly improved our own habits, and it was a real blessing to our family.

When to begin teaching about savings? Kindergarten is a great time. We give the children an allowance at this age and then teach them about saving. We talk about how they only get $5, but what if they saved their money for three months—then what could they buy? They get really excited about that when they think of the cool *big* toy they could get all on their own.

We then begin to set up a series of teaching and training opportunities for the children to learn about saving. We start by having them save 10 percent of their allowance. It's a great mind-set to have—pay the Lord His 10 percent and pay yourself 10 percent. It's a fantastic habit for them to get into, and it's not painful when it amounts to only fifty cents. In fact, when they're older we show them actuarial tables that show if they save 10 percent of their income their whole lives, they will end up as millionaires. That is highly motivational.

We next have the children set up a goal for saving. Parker set a goal to buy a video camera because he loved to make movies. He set up a picture of the camera he wanted along with the price, and we talked about and tracked his savings, keeping up the enthusiasm for the end goal. When he purchased the camera, we talked about how great it was that he had bought this all on his own and how good that must feel to him. And you better believe he takes care of it! It took him a long time to save the money for that camera, so he appreciates its value.

Another way to assist in the teaching of savings is by prim-ing the pump. Sometimes children just don't see the benefit of savings. You can see why. Saving fifty cents a week sure doesn't seem like a big deal. At that rate, it's hard for them to imagine ever reaching their savings goal. We add a few incentives to make saving more attractive, just to get them into the habit. This is done through the Bank of Boyack. The Bank of Boyack offers some great savings rates! Frankly, the thought of saving a dollar a month and getting a measly 1 percent interest doesn't sound all that exciting. So the Bank of Boyack offers much higher rates to make savings look much more enticing. To begin with, the Bank offers a 10 percent bonus upon reaching one's goal. So if the goal is $100, they get a $10 bonus when they hit their goal.

The Bank of Boyack also offers matched savings. For certain items, we will match dollar for dollar what the children save. Now, *that's* attractive! These plans really help the kids get excited about saving. Are they unrealistic? Sure. I'm still looking for a

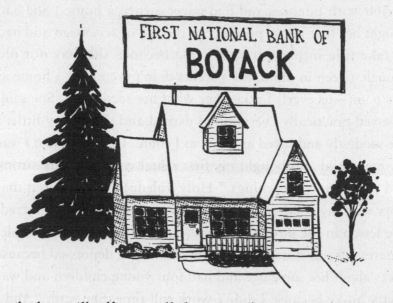

bank that will offer me all that! But this system does several things. It teaches the children to save. It teaches them about interest earnings (albeit on a greatly inflated scale). It teaches them to postpone gratification—rather than run out and spend all their money on candy, they can wait for something important. It also teaches them the Bit-by-Bit Principle, which is invaluable. That principle is simply that savings accumulate over time. Many people never learn this lesson and are impatient and always looking for a get-rich-quick scheme. (Okay, does the idea of multilevel marketing schemes ring a bell?) The Bit-by-Bit Principle is one of the most important lessons an adult can know. Those who understand it are the ones who end up as millionaires.

On the advertising flyer of the Bank of Boyack (okay, so we don't really have a flyer, but if we did have one it would have this) is the story of a client of mine. She was thirty-four years old when I met her and she was worth $3 million. This was more than ten years ago so that was (and is) a *lot* of money. She owned six homes, including the one her parents lived in. (They were terrible with finances and had never owned a home.) She had bought her first rental property at the age of *seventeen* and had to take title in her parents' name because she was not old enough. (Keep in mind, her parents didn't even *own* a home at this point—or ever!) I asked her what her secret was. She said, "I saved practically everything I earned and spent very little. I live modestly and saved as much as I could. I started when I was a young child and bought my first rental with my baby-sitting and part-time job earnings." Holy Toledo! I have shared that story with my children over and over and over. What an incredible lesson in the power of savings and the Bit-by-Bit Principle! (Interesting side note, at this point I'm feeling depressed because I was about her same age and had four young children and was pretty broke because I didn't work full-time. She said, "And I would trade it all to have a lovely family like yours." That brought me up short. I'm happy to report that she got married that year and now has two little ones. Oh, great, nice family *and* she's still rich!)

Mission/College Savings Matching Plan

Let me review how our matched savings plan works. This plan was created by my dad, so I call it the "Roger J. Browne Jr. Fantastically Effective Matched Savings Plan for Mission and/or College." He'd like that. He was a cool guy who would get such a bang out of knowing that people were using this. We'll call it Dad's Matched Savings Plan for short.

This is how The Plan works. For each dollar saved by the child toward a mission or college, the parent matches it with another dollar. This money is deposited into an account in a trust account for the child (under the child's Social Security number).

We sit our kids down when they turn eleven and talk about their future goals. We, of course, focus on saving for a mission.

My sister has both sons and daughters who used their funds to save for college and missions. Originally we started this at age twelve, but I've found that starting at eleven works better because they're still getting an allowance and it's easier for them to come up with the money. Then by the time they're twelve and their allowance drops out, they've acquired the habit.

The chart of contributions we're using currently is as follows:

Roger J. Browne Jr. Fantastically Effective Matched Savings Plan for Mission and/or College

AGE	AMOUNT/ MONTH	MATCH/ MONTH	PRINCIPAL SAVED
11	$ 8.00	$ 8.00	$ 192
12	16.00	16.00	384
13	25.00	25.00	600
14	37.00	37.00	888
15	50.00	50.00	1,200
16	70.00	70.00	1,680
17	100.00	100.00	2,400
18	160.00	160.00	3,840

TOTAL PRINCIPAL SAVED	$11,184
add interest earned	*1,000*
TOTAL AMOUNT SAVED	$12,184

So each month, your child gives you his or her share, you add to it your own, and you deposit it. The end total can vary depending on interest earned. This amount is enough for a mission or for a chunk of college or a wedding or whatever the goal is.

Clearly, at the beginning a simple savings account is the most functional. Most banks will provide a savings account to children with no monthly costs at all if you simply ask. Make sure to provide the *child's* Social Security number. Compare interest rates between banks.

Make sure your name is also on the account. When it becomes a larger amount, you will want to set up a custodial account. This is an account in your name as trustee for your child. This will also be set up under their Social Security number, not yours. You can set these up under various terms and titles—some are called UGMA's (Uniform Gift to Minors Account) or UTMA's (Uniform Trust Minors Account, I think). You can also pick an age for distribution. Usually age twenty-one is best—do *not* pick eighteen! That means that you control the money until that age.

After the amount begins to grow, you can use other investment alternatives such as mutual funds or bond funds. This is attractive when you have larger amounts of money (over $250). Some funds allow lower entry amounts (beginning balance) if it is a custodial account, so be sure to ask. Also, some funds may charge less. You may consider investing in life insurance policies for your child with an investment/interest component built into them. Some offer attractive interest rates, and they do provide a death benefit coverage for the child as well as guaranteed insurance for his or her whole life. People can usually add to these policies when they are older without having to meet any medical qualifications, and this is very attractive if they have health problems later in life. You need to shop for these wisely, as there are many products available. Make sure that you contact someone you trust and that you understand the policy completely. If it is too confusing, avoid the investment.

Remember, remember to *shop around* for investment rates. You will be surprised at the different rates and restrictions. Make sure you understand the investment *thoroughly,* and feel free to ask dumb questions as much as you want—it's your child's money! Better yet, have your child ask those dumb questions as well.

There are some options out there I'll talk about a little bit so you're exposed to them. You can invest in U.S. Savings Bonds. The interest is not taxable if used for a college education. The bonds need to be in your child's name and Social Security number.

Also, there are accounts called Coverdell ESA accounts that can be used to save for a child's education. They can be set up with any bank, financial institution, brokerage, or mutual fund company. The interest earned on these accounts is tax-free if the money is ultimately used for college education expenses. You set these up in your name as a trustee for your children and have a separate account for each child. You are restricted in the amount of contributions you can make each year, and there are also restrictions if your income as parents goes too high. If you are falling into these restrictions, please ask your financial advisor about the grandparent gift loophole to this one. Anyone can make gifts to this account, even grandparents, who may have a lower income than you.

Another type of account is a 529 plan. These are sponsored by the various states and can be used to save for college. An excellent Web site that compares these plans is <savingforcollege.com>. Please be aware that you do *not* have to invest in your own state's account. You can pick any one, but be very aware about how they will let you use the money. This is different from a Coverdell ESA in which you control the investments. These 529 plans have their investments controlled by their board of advisors. There are pros and cons to each, so investigate carefully. And by all means have your children do the investigating with you! Have them type in these terms on the Internet, and you can research things out together. From time to time, my son would call me and say, "I've been studying the market and I want to move my money here." Incredible.

Another option for mission savings is a custodial account with a mutual fund. This has a different twist. The other accounts I just discussed have to be used for education and not missions. So be careful where you put their money. If you invest in a mutual fund or stocks, you can do the following. My son Connor invested in a mutual fund. It happened to be during the time when such investments were making like 75 percent a year! It was crazy. (You want a good lesson on savings? Every time he got his statement, he would run around the house screaming how he had earned $350 for doing absolutely nothing. My kids got hooked on savings after that.) So it came time for his mission. If we had liquidated and sold out the mutual fund, he would have been looking at declaring all that income for tax purposes. Instead, we contacted the Church's Missionary Department. We got the number for their mutual fund account with the same company and had a direct transfer made, transferring all the money from Connor's account directly to the Church's account. This way, he had no income tax hit whatsoever because it was a direct charitable donation. Cool, eh? And that's all perfectly fine with the Church and aboveboard.

Now let's talk about some nitty-gritties on how this savings plan works and what it does. We look at the year as a whole, so if the children want to use birthday or Christmas money to pay a chunk toward their matched savings, that's fine. Also, they may make more money in the summer, and so the savings schedule may be loaded to that time frame. Sometimes they put their whole clothing budget or part of it toward their savings obligation, then just buy clothes with their own supplemental earnings whenever they want. All of this is good flexibility and works well. The bottom line is that they are meeting this obligation on an annual basis. Don't let them get very far behind because they don't have the earning capacity to catch up, and it becomes a hairy issue. We start out, however, very carefully getting the amount each month for several years until they are in the proper mind-set and habit.

So do I meticulously put in that $6 or $12 a month? Sometimes. Sometimes I let it pile up and then stick in a chunk. We are sticklers with the kids but cut ourselves some slack in getting the money over to the accounts. (Don't tell the kids.) It's probably better, really, not to let yourself get behind either!

What's amazing is what this plan does. Just think about it. Your kids will be making a multiyear commitment to saving. They will be committing every month: "I'm going on a mission and to college." Or "I'm saving for college and a temple marriage." The value of that recurring commitment cannot be over-stressed. It is a fantastic lesson. It teaches them about saving, about investing, about dedication, and about budgeting. It is incredible.

Now, you may hit the sixteen-year-old bump in the road. When your child turns sixteen, he will have over $3,000 saved. This becomes suddenly very attractive and significant. You will probably get the statement, "Hey, that's *my* money and I want to buy a car!" Prepare for this day way ahead of time so you don't get blindsided. We've handled it as follows: "Son, first of all, half of that money is ours." (They seem to always conveniently forget that part.) "That money has been set aside to pay for your mission. It is sacred, dedicated money. It is for the Lord. It cannot be used to pay for a car." Now you may get this reaction (which we've gotten every time): "Well, fine, then I'm not going on a mission and I'm taking my part out to buy a car." (Lest you think my children are all evil, Connor finished a mission in Honduras and the others are—knock on wood—planning on theirs. They just get argumentative. They all take the "yack" in "Boyack" quite seriously.)

Then you drop the bomb. "Son, if you do not go on a mission, then this money will be used to support another missionary who cannot afford to go. It is sacred money and it will be used only for missionary work." There is some grumbling, but that usually ends the discussion.

Now, for daughters, you will need to revise this dialogue somewhat unless planning for a mission has been a serious component of the savings. "Daughter, this money is being saved for college and temple marriage. It is dedicated to that and to your future. If you choose not to use it for those things, then we will donate it to truly needy children in Africa so they can go to school." Did you hear that freight train coming to a screeching halt? End of discussion.

Again, may I bear testimony? This plan has worked incredibly well with my brother, nieces, nephews, and my own kids. It has been a tremendous blessing to my family. You know, it's interesting. Compare our son who has worked since the age of eleven, carefully saving for his mission, to the boy whose parents just automatically pay for the mission when he turns nineteen. Who values the mission experience more? Who is more careful with his money? In fact, Connor told me he saved even *more* money while he was on his mission by saving gifts from relatives. Compare that to the missionaries who are burning through their monthly allotment and crying home for more and more money. My father-in-law commented that during the entire six years he was bishop, only one boy saved for his mission. The rest were paid for by parents or the ward.

Look at my nieces, who paid for a major portion of their college with their savings. They are now young married women, and guess what? They budget amazingly well. They're frugal and stay out of debt. They have savings allocated for the various things they need. I cannot ever overstate the impact of this program. You will receive abundant and incredible blessings that will affect generations of your family. Okay, was that big enough?

Granted, this works well if you start young. But you might have children who are already in the middle of those teen years. It's time for some really frank and open discussions. Sit your teens down *today* and discuss their future. Have them make a budget for college and mission and maybe wedding savings. Make sure they stick in everything—have you priced college textbooks lately? It will freak them out, so be prepared. (Of course, it may freak you out too.) Then talk about how you as a family will meet this obligation. You need to burst that balloon of, "Gee, I thought you guys were going to pay for all of this!" Here's a good response: "You know what, as soon as someone gives me a couple of million bucks I'll take that under consideration. Until then, let us rejoin the real world." The earlier you can have this conversation, the better. All of a sudden, scholarships and good grades really become attractive.

We also need to talk about the day that comes when they refuse to contribute their amount to the savings plan. Ah, happy day. It usually hits around age fourteen, the same year they begin their mutation process into a monosyllabic vegetable. How do you handle this? Creatively and persistently. We sit them down and have a reality-check conversation. Sometimes we have to have a few of those conversations. We review their future expenses. They often reach that bail point: "Fine, I won't do *anything*." Do *not* react to that. Just calmly say, "Well, that is one option. But in our family, we are committed to this." They'll react: "Well, then, I'll move to a different family." Why is it that fourteen-year-olds always threaten this? We try to encourage them to go ahead and move, but so far they have all chosen to stay. Frankly, I don't think they could ever find anyone to take them in! Ha!

What if that doesn't work? Well, we've had to *strongly*

encourage participation from time to time. "Honey, we can see that you're strapped, so we'll apply your clothing budget to get you caught up" (or birthday money or whatever).

"What? I *need* that money!"

"Well, do you have any other ideas?" We do not ever let this drop. They cannot wear us down. We are absolutely committed to this as a family, so they learn that it will never go away. Creativity and persistence. Do *not* give up.

Give your kids the gift of expecting them to pay a major chunk of their post-age-eighteen expenses. We have friends who believed in paying for their kids' missions and college. Now, after their child has bombed through two years of college and gotten booted out, they have begun to rethink that strategy. They've seen our boy say, "Man, I've got to get back to studying. If I don't pass this class, it'll cost me a thousand dollars." Bravo!

Can you help out? Sure. But keep it small. Our policy is to pay for housing for the first year of college and books the second. That's it. Shocking, eh? We may send a little here and there, but it's not much and it's extremely random.

Remember, what is our end goal? Independence. This needs to be approached in steps. As they begin to pay for tuition, rent, and food, they suddenly become aware of budgeting, saving, and penny-pinching. Do not deprive your children of these excellent lessons. Even if you can afford to pay for everything, do you really want to handicap your children by delaying their life education for many years? It is interesting that the parents who criticize my husband and me for raising our children with frugality and having them help pay their way are the same parents who gripe and complain that their kids are burning through the money and always calling for more and haven't saved a dime and don't ever keep a job.

Do our kids complain? Oh, no, not our lovelies. They walk around saying, "Oh, Mother and Father dear, thank you so much for the wonderful lessons of thrift and savings you are teaching us. We know that this will bless our lives and could save our marriages. We know that we are learning to value everything we have. Thanks again. We feel the love!" Oh, sure. They say that right after they clean their rooms to a spotless shine and offer to help us with anything we need.

Of *course* they complain! And we keep saying, "Someday you will thank us." And now the oldest brother writes to his younger brothers and says, "Guys, lay off Mom and Dad. You would not believe how great it is to understand all this stuff. I'm having to deal with all these flaky guys who can't handle their money at all." That helps.

Again, I testify that this plan will bless your family. Commit to it and stick to it, and it will have tremendous results.

Investment Training

When you moved out of your parents' house, were you an expert on investment alternatives? How was your understanding of compound interest? We can all chuckle about this because about 99.5 percent of us were clueless about investment and about 50 percent of us still are.

Adults cannot be truly independent until they understand how their money works and how they can make it work. Until then, they are ignorant and dependent. So let's move ahead and arm our children (and perhaps ourselves!) with great information and learning that will give them an incredible advantage over others.

I'll start with the end of the story. We got a call from our son who was in his first year at BYU. We said, "What's up?" He said, "Well, I just finished teaching all my roommates about mutual funds. We've been looking over the various investment possibilities on the Internet and they're all deciding where to put their savings. These guys all had their money in stupid little savings accounts getting about 1 percent. Isn't that dumb? So anyway, they're all calling their parents right now to talk to them about it and invest their money better." That is absolutely true. My hubby and I looked at each other in shock. Then we did the Dance of Joy and high-fived each other. Yes! It worked!

Teaching your children about investing begins when they are age five. Yes, you read it right: age five. That's when you start talking about interest. Of course, at that age, we call it the Big Savings Reward! We teach them they get a reward if they save. They think there's this magical Saving Fairy that gives them this reward. But they begin to understand it very simply.

As their own investments change, their education grows with these changes. So we begin to call interest by its true name about the time they hit third grade. We tell them how it really works. We have them set up a little savings account at the local bank. (They're free!) We show them their statements monthly and have them check things out. We also begin at this age to talk about stocks and how they work.

Their best learning will come from actual experience. Go ahead and buy them a savings bond and let them see how it works. Have Grandma buy them stock for a Christmas present and let them track it. (The Disney stock certificate is darling!) Show them how to compare rates at various banks and have *them* decide where to put their account.

One Christmas, we gave our teenage son an E*Trade account with a balance in it for him to invest. Much better than cash. How great it is for them to make these decisions and learn with small amounts of money that they don't need to feed their family. Most of us learn these lessons right in the middle of our lives when we're desperately trying to feed our families and save for retirement. How much better would it be if we had experience before then?

Have a family home evening lesson on the stock market. Get out the *Wall Street Journal* and the business section of the newspaper. Then give each child $5,000 in Monopoly money and tell them they can invest it in any stocks they want. Have them put together their own "Investment Portfolio" and track it over the next three to six months. Put a chart on the fridge tracking everybody's portfolio values. They absolutely love it when they beat Mom and Dad! Can you see the great lessons they learn? Did you know what a price/earnings ratio was? Did you know about fiscal years and dividends? These terms will grow to make sense to your kids as they study their "own" investments.

There are a couple of great resources I want to direct you to. The first is the personal management merit badge book from the Boy Scouts. You can buy one at your local Scout office for about three dollars, and it is one of the best investments you can make in your child's investment education. We use this at about age thirteen with the kids. If you have sons, that's great—they can earn the merit badge! If you have daughters—fantastic! Let them "earn" it as well. Go through each of the requirements and study this book in detail together as a family. It is an incredible resource and written to kids this age.

When we go on vacation (which is often an extended road trip with camping), we generally take along a merit badge or two to work on. This one is a great one for that. As we're driving through those lovely portions of Nevada or New Mexico or wherever, we pull out the book and begin. Luckily, I have a degree in business/finance so I know most of the terms and information to be able to teach. You may need to study in advance if you don't. Each hour we have a short discussion on the various items listed. What is simple interest? What is compound interest? What is the difference? The book then describes most of these terms. We let the older ones (who know absolutely everything, they believe) teach the things they know to the younger ones. This is a great reinforcement for their learning as well, and it keeps them involved even if they already have earned the badge and know the material. They love puffing up their chest and pontificating on the various merits of investing in stocks vs. bonds. Mom and Dad take turns as well. We then have a reward for finishing each section: money to buy treats at the next pit stop, or DVD time.

When we worked through this merit badge for the third time, my hubby turned to me and said, "Man, I feel like I've earned a degree in financial planning after this!" Like I said, teaching this to your children will benefit you as well. We're about to do it for the fourth and probably final time this month on our family vacation. Due to the spacing of our kids, it has ended up being about every three years. I'm delighted that it will be reinforced once again for the older boys and that they can talk intelligently to the youngest about their own personal experiences with interest and investing.

Part of the merit badge is keeping a ninety-day budget. This part is fantastic! If you don't yet have a budget yourself, offer to do it with the kids at the same time. And yes, even if they're not earning the merit badge, you can have them do that particular requirement.

So go get the book today. Even if you only read it for yourself!

Another great resource is a Web site, <Quicken.com>. This is a fantastic Web site with an amazing amount of financial information. Have your kids (and yourself!) become familiar with it. There are all kinds of calculators in there. Have your kids punch in the info. "If we buy a car at 5 percent interest and put $3,000 down, is that better than buying it with the loan from the credit union at 7 percent with no money down?" Have them put the figures in, and the Web site will compare the alternatives for you. Have them use it for their own learning as well. "Judy, can you study up on what a Certificate of Deposit is and report to the family at next family home evening? And why don't you compare three banks in the area and tell us which one has the best offer." They can do mini-reports at your family business meeting (we have one a month). Have them all compare their investment portfolios as well.

What's weird is that they love this stuff—especially if it is *real*. If you're really buying a car or if Grandpa is really going to set up a CD, it is exhilarating. I still remember my son discussing his mutual fund investments with Grandma, who didn't know what a mutual fund was. Make it as real as you can and the kids will get hooked. This is big-time real adult stuff and it's *money* and it's important and they know it.

The biggest lesson for kids to see in investing is the power of compound interest. This is the reality of the Bit-by-Bit Principle. I'll share with you my favorite example. It shows that if you save $2,000 a year throughout your twenties and then stop and *never save another dime,* you will end up with over twice as much money as someone who starts at age forty and saves $2,000 a year for *twenty-five years*. And you only saved for ten years.

Now *that* is a powerful example of the power of savings. We review that over and over and over. Have them punch in some scenarios into savings calculators they find on the Internet and experiment on their own.

There are a number of books and pamphlets out there on this topic. Look for college textbooks, which are geared toward teaching the subject. There is also tremendous information on the Internet. Tell your daughter, "Can you check out which has better rates and fees, E*Trade or Ameritrade, and let me know?" They're a whiz at this stuff—let them shine!

I think one of your greatest resources is people. Have your parents or grandparents talk to the children about the Depression and what it really was like. Have Uncle Dave talk about his investment portfolio. Have Cousin Suzie tell them what it was like to get buried in credit card debt in her college years and how long it took to dig out. Get them their own (very understanding) financial planner and let them make appointments to review their investments. Have them talk to the banker themselves. Have their advisors at church talk about these topics. Here again, having many voices teaching these things will ring into their brains much better than Mom and Dad's lectures. Have older siblings talk with younger ones or nieces or nephews who are investing. Take them to those free lectures you see advertised. Have them go talk to the speakers on life insurance as an investment vehicle. Cool!

Now, some kids will get into this more seriously than others. Some will get into it later. But if it is real enough, they all will join in eventually. Sometimes it won't kick in until your sixteen-year-old decides he really, really needs a motorcycle. "Sure!" you say as he falls off the edge of the chair. "Why don't you shop around and see what's available?" He shops, shops, shops. Then you use this as an opportunity. "Okay, tell me what you've learned." You'll be amazed. "Okay, now how about financing? Why don't you check that out?" Suddenly the kid is learning about loans, interest, down payments, collateral, and that lovely law that says you can't enter into a contract until age eighteen. Ha! Use these opportunities for learning. You could say, "Are you nuts! I'm never buying a motorcycle and you're never owning one as long as you're under our roof!" Instead, go with the flow. Have him or her research and learn. The end result—no child of mine will own a motorcycle until he is eighteen and independent—will eventually come on its own. But now, it's not Mom being an ogre. It's the law and it's the finances. And meanwhile, incredible lessons of investing and saving and borrowing money have been learned. Use them!

Borrowing Issues

Equally important to teaching about savings and investing is teaching about borrowing. Frankly, the 1980s message of "Just Say No!" will not cut it. You are wasting your breath when you lecture, "Now, sweetheart, credit cards are a tool of the devil. Stay away from them." Sure, that ought to work. Until she gets that envelope in the mail addressed personally to her (so exciting!) and it really is a great card and she's not really going to *use* it, she just wants to have it for emergencies. And away you go.

In order to be independent, a young adult needs a working knowledge of borrowing. A prepared young adult is a safe young adult.

The prophet has clearly counseled us on this matter: "We have been counseled again and again concerning self-reliance, concerning debt, concerning thrift. So many of our people are heavily in debt for things that are not entirely necessary. When I was a young man, my father counseled me to build a modest

113

home, sufficient for the needs of my family, and make it beautiful and attractive and pleasant and secure. He counseled me to pay off the mortgage as quickly as I could so that, come what may, there would be a roof over the heads of my wife and children. I was reared on that kind of doctrine. I urge you as members of this Church to get free of debt where possible and to have a little laid aside against a rainy day" (Gordon B. Hinckley, "The Times in Which We Live," *Ensign*, November 2001, 73).

Frankly, when I hear the prophet say "counseled again and again," that kind of catches my attention. We must do a thorough job of teaching our children these principles to avoid their future bondage by debt.

When our kids get to be about age eleven or twelve, we begin to discuss credit and paying interest. They are perfectly capable of understanding at this point, and so we set up a great learning experience. At around this age, they want bigger, cooler stuff. We let them pick something big and cool and expensive, usually something like a stereo or a bike. We then say, "Honey, the Bank of Boyack would be delighted to make you a loan." They're flabbergasted. "Really?" "Absolutely," we say. Then we enter into loan negotiations. We talk about collateral. ("And if you don't pay, we get to keep your CD player, which we will sell on eBay." Bless eBay.) We talk to them about interest to be charged (and we make it *painful;* minimum is 20 percent). We talk about payments. Then we set up a promissory note (you can get forms on the Internet or make up a simple one of your own) and we have them sign it. And away we go.

This lesson works so well because they usually absolutely hate it. They get to really resent those payments and the reminders that they will lose their collateral. They despise paying the interest—which we point out with glee. ("Look, honey, we just made five bucks for doing nothing! Woo-hoo!" Mom and Dad high-five each other.)

You usually have to teach this lesson only once. It makes an indelible impression on a child's mind about how horrible it is to be in debt. But sometimes mini-lessons along the way work well to reinforce this concept.

Dad: "Sure, I'll loan you $5, but you have to pay me $10 by Saturday."

Suzie: "But that's highway robbery!"

Dad: "Take it or leave it."

Suzie: "But I really want to go to the movies."

Dad: "Sounds great, do we have a deal?"

Suzie: "Fine."

Come Saturday. Dad: "Pay up, you owe me $10."

Suzie: "Daaaad. That's so not fair."

Dad: "Yup."

Grumbling ensues. Payment is made. Dad goes skipping to Mom for their high-five party, "Look, I got $5 from Suzie for loaning money. Woo-hoo."

This is a strange teaching experience. You want your children to so despise having to pay interest that by the time they are eighteen, those credit cards do not appeal to them. They've learned how much it really costs and how awful it is to have debt hanging over their heads. The very best way is for them to have experience with what debt really is. And you want it to be a lousy experience, so be sure to construct it that way. None of this, "Boy, Mom and Dad only charged me 2 percent interest. This loan business is great!"

Debt is a serious problem. The prophet has spoken about it repeatedly. It is crippling many, many people in the world. To quote Roman playwright Publilius Syrus, "Debt is the slavery of the free."

These lessons must be taught with clarity. Children usually won't learn how paying interest works unless they experience it. They must be taught the difference between "reasonable debt" (mortgage, car loan) and "unwise debt" (credit cards, consumer debt). So teach them all about what a mortgage is and how it works. If you're refinancing your house, have them go along with you and talk about it.

As important as the lesson on compound interest was when they were learning about investments, the lesson on compound interest as it relates to borrowing is even more important. Have them do the math. Have them "charge" a CD or a pair of shoes and then calculate how much it would take to pay it off in a year's time on the credit card with compound interest. It is incredible. They need to *see* those numbers and calculate them on their own. Just talking in the abstract will go in one ear and out the other.

Again, lessons learned by other people can be shared, and those stories will stick with the kids. They'll never forget hearing about how Grandpa, after going through the Depression, has always paid cash and is as free as a bird and doesn't owe a soul. They'll never forget how Cousin Louis stuck his motorcycle on a credit card and ended up paying five times what it cost and could have had *five* motorcycles. Having them hear stories—the good and the bad—from real-life experiences will stick with them. Caution here: do not dwell on your own negative experiences. Children need to feel security from their parents, and they will lose this completely if you spill all about your desperate circumstances. Do *not* burden them with your current adult concerns.

Most important, bear your testimony about following the prophet and his counsel to avoid debt. That is powerful counsel, and they need to know you're living it.

Budgeting Issues

Euuww. The dreaded *budget* word. I use this term to describe all those day-to-day expenses we deal with. How can we share these experiences and understandings with the kids? First of all, we need to be a bit open about things. They need to know what is involved; we can't keep everything a secret.

For us, the best way to start is the Monopoly family home evening. We start with a huge pile of money representing how much money the family brings in. We usually do not tell what this amount is—remember Sally running to school with that juicy information? But we have the pile with the actual amount of income. And use all those 1s and 5s and 10s—not the big bills. It looks like an amazing amount. We then begin by telling the kids that we're going to plan our budget and that they get to spend the money. We ask, "Now what would you like to do with this huge pile of money?" "Go to Disneyland!" "Buy new bikes for everyone!" "I could use it all for clothes!"

"That sounds fun!" we say. "But first we have to pay our bills." They all agree to that.

"So what do we pay first?" Of course, they come up with tithing, which we have them pay. And they just about croak when they see how much it is. Another brief testimony on tithing can be shared. Then we ask them what other bills we have to pay. Our mortgage comes out—and that takes forever to count out. Then they go on naming about half a dozen others—food, car, orthodontist (who I think is enjoying his summer home paid for by the work he did on my four kids). Then they can't think of anything else and are delighted that there is still a big pile left.

That's when the education begins. "What about the lights?" Oh, yeah, those dreaded utility bills! "What about insurance?" You mean you have to actually *pay* for health insurance? Talk about life insurance as well, which they often know nothing about. And what in the world is car registration? And on and on it goes.

Be *sure* to keep firing the bills at them until they have run out of money, and then still keep firing the bills at them. "We need a new roof. We need to save for retirement."

They begin to protest, "But we're out of money!"

"Well, we need to put that roof on, don't we? And don't you still want to go to Disneyland?"

It is amazing to watch the understanding that dawns upon them. Some will begin to get a little worried and upset. "But how will we make it?"

Then you begin phase two. "Well, how could we save money to be able to meet those bills?" We compare how much it costs to make dinner with how much it costs to take the family to McDonald's. We ask how they could help. They become interested in actually turning off the lights, and we translate that into savings to get the family to Disneyland. We write up an action plan for cutting back expenses. It is a great process.

We have done this every few years with the kids—annually when they were younger. It is an amazing tool for teaching about budgeting and pinching pennies and making ends meet. It is also a great tool to prepare them for what it means to have a family. All of a sudden, they're not really content with that career plan of being a professional mountain biker.

A follow-up to this is to have *them* pay the bills. This shows up in The Plan that was discussed in chapter 3, and you may have wondered what that was. We keep our budgeting and checking accounts on a software program called *Quicken,* which I highly, highly recommend. For a few months when they reach that age on The Plan, we have them actually pay the bills (or enter in the automatic ones) and balance the family checkbook. Talk about enlightening. They then start getting after the family: "We can't order pizza again. I need that money to pay the water bill!" It's rather funny. Again, this is an adult activity, so most kids are intrigued. For the less-than-motivated, I've been tempted to offer them, say, 1 percent of anything they don't use for the bills. I figure 1 percent of zero is no great amount—ha! Here again, this is a very *real* experience that will stay with them forever.

After they have this experience and pass off this part of The Plan, we talk quite openly with the older ones about our bills. We ask their opinions and keep them in the loop about upcoming expenses. By now they're old enough to keep things private, and the educational aspects are excellent.

Once they get familiar with *Quicken,* we have them set up their own budget. The older kids track their own expenses and accounts on it as well. They have their own checking accounts by age sixteen, with their own debit cards. We give them lunch money or other things the family pays for in big chunks into their accounts that they then have to manage and budget.

Can you see how amazing this is? And frankly, it's rather fun. Compare a child who has this understanding and experience at the age of eighteen with yourself and what you knew at that age. Light-years difference in my case! I can still remember my sister showing me how to fill out a check when I began college. Ah, so clueless. It was a miracle I didn't go through financial disaster. The sad part is that so many do because no one ever taught them.

Wow, we've talked a *ton* about financial education for our independent-kids-in-training. I hope your mind has been expanded as to how important this is, and that you have gotten many ideas for how to go about it. This training is crucial for your children to be truly independent. Make the commitment to give them this gift.

> Money, money, money!
> The more you teach,
> The more they'll learn;
> The more they learn,
> The more they'll earn;

The more they earn,
The more they'll save;
The more they save,
The happier they'll be—
So let's teach about money to every child!

CHAPTER 7

Using the Family to Help Train the Kids

Let's play *So You Want to Be a PARENT!* (Cue the music from *Who Wants to Be a Millionaire?*)

Disclaimer—There is no financial compensation for this game—but that's pretty much true of parenting as well.

So, let's go! Who wants to play?

First question, for 100 mental sanity points:

You are traveling on a plane alone with a baby and a toddler. You lift the baby up as the food is served over to the toddler's tray. The gentleman behind you taps you on the shoulder to tell you that the baby has barfed in your hair. What do you do?

a. Thank the gentleman, hand *him* the baby, and go to the rest room to clean up.

b. Laugh out loud for a while, put the baby on the floor, put all the food trays on your toddler's tray, encourage the toddler not to eat all the food, lean forward and try to mop up the mess on your head with all the napkins and an extra diaper.

c. Whisk out the hat you packed just in case such a thing would occur and put it on your head.

d. Begin to cry uncontrollably.

To quote Anonymous: "Laugh and the whole world laughs with you. Cry and you . . . will sink into a deep depression, put on twenty more pounds, and *still* have changed nothing." Okay, so maybe I modified that quote a bit.

You may have guessed that the first question was based on my own real-life experience, one of those wonderful trips when I was traveling with a baby and toddler. I chose "b." To quote "famous parenting expert" Ed Asner, "Raising kids is part joy and part guerrilla warfare."

The family unit is the perfect environment for training children. You have constant interactions, a forum for setting an example, and many opportunities for teaching and training. Plus, you can use the family itself for promoting this training.

In this chapter we're going to talk about a few things related specifically to family life that you can use to reach your goals of raising independent children. Feel free to adapt these ideas at will for your own individual family.

Establish Family Identity

If someone were to describe your family, what three words would they use? Okay, not *dysfunctional, dangerous,* and *weird*—those are mine! But seriously, how would someone who knows your family describe you? If I had to guess, the three words (other than those listed above) to describe my family would be *Mormon, Scouters, techno wienies.* Okay, that's four words, but only three categories, so it's fine. There may be others, but these are probably the big three.

So how would someone describe your family? Musical? Sportsy? Political? Animal lovers? Drama people? Motorcyclists? It's rather interesting to contemplate. Each family has its own identity and uniqueness. No two families are exactly alike. Let me share some examples. Our neighbors would be sportsy, traveling Catholics. (Man, that sounds like some weird rock group!) My girlfriend's family are car nuts, Mormon, sci-fi junkies.

(Now, that *has* to be a singing group.) You may wonder what the point is. Bear with me.

Some of this family identity will be planned; some will evolve in the family over time. For example, my hubby and I definitely planned on having a Scouting family. My dad and brother were big Scouters, and I loved it. In fact, every guy I dated I would ask, "Are you an Eagle Scout?" If they said no, I'd end up dropping them. My hubby had his Eagle Scout *and* three palms (that means fifteen extra merit badges) *and* had worked at Scout camp for three summers. It was love at first sight! Lucky for us, the good Lord was extremely cooperative and sent four boys into our family, and we became quite the avid Scouters. So this was a planned family identity.

Other family identities will evolve over time. Libby's family is becoming a missionary family as all of her five sons are either coming home from or going on missions. Carmen's family has become an artistic family since the children began to develop a love for art that spread to the parents.

Make your family identity broad enough so that everyone will fit into it. For example, "We're the creative family" can work for Sally, who paints beautifully, and Sam, who cooks like a master. "We're the reading family" can include everyone from Dad, who loves spy novels, to Jose, who adores Harry Potter.

What is the point of all this? You can use your family identity to teach your children independence and your family's values and morals. It serves as a framework for instruction. You can hang many lessons onto this identity framework for what I call "stealth teaching."

For example, let's say you are a sports family. You love to watch and participate in sports. How can you use that identity to teach your children independence? Well, let's look at the lessons that can be taught with sports participation:

1. Perseverance—this one is a no-brainer

    2. Dependability

    3. Commitment

    4. Teamwork and cooperation

    5. Striving for excellence and not compromising

    6. Motor skills and ability

    7. Health and nutrition

    8. Compassion

I could go on and on. Isn't it amazing? And you thought they were just having fun playing Little League.

Let's take one more example. Let's take a family who is known for its dedication to The Church of Jesus Christ of Latter-day Saints. The neighbors say, "Yeah, they're the Mormons." (I always chuckle when someone moves in and seems to hear in a nanosecond that we're LDS. It's usually the first thing that pops out of their mouth after "hello.") So what can be taught from that family identity?

    1. Missionary work

    2. Tolerance and understanding for others

    3. Integrity

    4. Charity

    5. Setting a good example

    6. Commitment

    7. Radiating love

Again, we could add much, much more.

So the family identity serves to teach many of the principles and behaviors that your children will need to master to become outstanding, independent adults. And throughout this learning/teaching process, they are acquiring knowledge and wisdom that they don't even know they're being taught! That's why this is "stealth teaching" at its best.

You can also layer items from The Plan into the family identity model to be passed off. Be creative with this and have fun. Say, for example, you want your child to pass off baking a cake, learning how to use tools, and cleaning his room. How can you use your family identity as science fiction buffs to make those rather bland and boring tasks seem more fun and interesting? Well, have the child bake a cake and decorate it like a spaceship. Blue frosting is very appealing to most children. Rather than saying, "You have to bake a cake," say, "You get to create a spaceship and here are all your materials." Wild horses couldn't drag your techno child away from the task.

The children need to learn to use tools? Give them tons of scrap wood and metal and say, "Go make me a Borg." (Translation for the science-fiction impaired: a Borg is a cybernetic life form—lots of machine parts on a gray-looking, creepy guy. One of the first phrases my children learned was, "Space . . . the final frontier. These are the voyages of the Starship Enterprise." They could recite the whole intro to *Star Trek* at about the age of two.)

They need to clean their room? Have them decorate their room like the bridge of a starship. Then tell them they need to clean it and have it inspected by the captain. Illustrate with an

example on the TV: "Do you see lots of stuff on the floor of the bridge of the ship? What would happen if there was a mess? Can you imagine the captain tripping over all this stuff in the middle of an attack by the Borg? Or what if they hit anti-gravity? All the stuff piled on your dresser and bed would go whipping around the room and knock somebody out! Let's get this room so clean that it can survive going through anti-gravity." Okay, by now your children think you're a nut case and they're giggling. But guess what? You walk in and say, "I'm the captain, and we're under attack. How clean is my bridge?" You bet they'll be thinking about it when they're cleaning, and even though it's silly, they'll strive to get their bedroom "bridge" looking like the spotless TV version.

The possibilities of incorporating your family identity are endless. You are teaching to the child's strengths and using them to accomplish your goal of fostering independence.

Let's work through one more example. Your family identity is good shoppers. Don't laugh. This is so totally my friend Diane. She is an absolute artist when it comes to shopping, and the rest of the family is following suit. So let's say you need to teach your fourteen-year-old daughter interior designing principles, car engine understanding, and resume preparation. Two out of three of these—and perhaps all three—may be a tough sell. So let's use the family identity to teach them. Again, creativity and fun are key.

"Brynn, you need to learn interior designing principles this year, so we're going to let you redecorate your room. It'll be like on that TV show, only your budget will be $200 and you'll have two weeks. You need to go shopping and get everything you need." Now, as you take her shopping, you begin to teach. "It's best to have a balance of color and texture. What is your color scheme, and what do you want to get to bring in texture?" You take her around the store and show her fabrics, paint, wood, and so on to teach her all about those elements of design. She's whipping around the store happy as a clam and has no idea she's learning a ton about interior design. "It's good to add living things into a room to give it life and color. What do you want to use?" She's shopping around the backyard for plants to stick in. And away she goes. Compare that to Mom sitting down with an interior design book and lecturing . . . snoring ensues. But stick that girl in a store and you can teach your brains out and she just thinks she's shopping!

On to understanding a car engine. Oh, now you're just snickering and wondering how I'm going to be able to work this one out. Aha, creativity rules. "Honey, a car engine is just like a big shopping mall. Here you have the oil. That's like the ATM that keeps the whole system running. If there weren't an ATM, the whole mall would seize up. The dipstick is used to check the balance and see if you need more cash in the machine. Now here's how you check your balance." Aren't you impressed? On we go, "This is the radiator. It's like the giant air conditioning system in the mall. If the air conditioning blew out, everyone would be steaming mad and leave and the whole mall would shut down." And on we could go, describing the engine in terms she understands completely and likes. She'll be laughing halfway through and making up stuff along with you. She'll never look at a car engine quite the same way ever again.

Resume preparation is easy, but talk about a dull task. How could you liven it up? One day, when you're at her favorite store, ask her if she would like to work there someday because the employees get a 15 percent discount. You now have her complete and undivided attention. "Yes, they even get 15 percent off of the sale and clearance stuff." Now she is downright riveted. You go home, plop her in front of the computer, and say, "Let's put together your resume as if you were applying for that job. What skills do you have that would make you an attractive employee?"

Well, she is a veteran shopper and has a deep understanding of pricing, placement, marketing, and so forth. She's hooked in.

Go to where the child's strengths are and build from there, layering in tasks that need to be done. By all means, have a ton of fun with this! They may think you're nuts, but they'll be having a ball and learning a lot in the process.

Develop Family Mottos

After you have an understanding of your family identity, another element that can help with The Plan is to develop your own family mottos. These are like mini mission statements.

We have several family mottos:

"Boyacks are early."

"Boyacks don't bail."

"Boyacks live the Scout Law."

"Boyacks follow the prophet."

"Boyacks decorate like nuts for holidays—especially Christmas!"

The development of these mottos has taken years of being a family.

We began with "Boyacks are early." This was because "Brownes are late." My family growing up was *always* late. We always came in after the meeting had started and had to squeeze in the back. We were always in a rush to get places because we had waited until the last minute to get ready. And I hated it. So when I got married, I decided that my family was going to be early. It was just as easy to be ten minutes early as it was to be ten minutes late. It was just a matter of making the decision. And so, "Boyacks are early" was created. And we are! People know that we'll be there sitting in place ten minutes early. As a result, the whole family is programmed to accomplish that, and several principles have been taught, such as preparedness, courtesy, and commitment.

"Boyacks don't bail" came from our being very involved parents. My hubby and I are quite involved in many commitments to work, community, and church. And one of the things that absolutely drove us crazy was people who were irresponsible. The worst ones were the ones who said they would do something and then would bail out and not do it. Hence, as we were teaching these principles of dependability and reliability to our children, we coined the motto, "Boyacks don't bail." When our kids wanted to bomb out on something, we merely had to say this family motto. They would feel practically compelled to finish because *that's who we are.*

The Scout Law motto came after the four sons did. What a great way to sum up that we choose to live as people of integrity! So when Son acts grumpy, we say, "Boyacks live the Scout Law." Bingo. Understanding is instantaneous. No big ol' hairy lecture is needed. The Scout Law has been modified in our home to be, "A *Boyack* is trustworthy, loyal, helpful, friendly, courteous, kind, cheerful, thrifty, brave, clean, and reverent." Whew! That covers a ton! So rather than going into a harangue on the importance of a cheerful attitude, we encapsulate: "Boyacks live the Scout Law." Done.

Following the prophet is huge in our family and probably the single guiding principle of spirituality. This was reinforced by a family experience that profoundly and permanently affected our family. My husband got laid off in the recession of 1994. It was a terrible time to get laid off because absolutely nobody was hiring. We had a family home evening and announced to the family that this had happened and that it may be a long time before Daddy could find another job. My children were instantly afraid. "What will this mean? How will we live?" and the little one piped up, "How will we get food to eat?" At that point, we stood them all up and marched them into the kitchen and opened the pantry door. I said, "Kids, we have a year's supply of food. Look at all this food! In fact, we have a year's supply of paper towels and garbage bags and tons of stuff. We'll be fine."

We have always had a year's supply; they were just used to it and didn't realize what that meant. My husband said, "Boys, the prophet has told us to have a year's supply. Now we've done that and the Lord will bless us." Steve was out of work for more than ten months, and our supply lasted through it all. Practically every day the children would pray, "We're thankful for our prophet who told us to store food."

So what to others was merely a nice thing to do became a defining characteristic and belief in our home. My children literally felt that the prophet had saved our family—which he had. Following the prophet is our spiritual driving force.

We use this principle a *lot* with our teenagers. We study the *For the Strength of Youth* pamphlet like scriptures in our family, and that has come to equal the prophet's voice. So when an issue comes up, such as appropriate music, we can merely say, "Boyacks follow the prophet," and it is understood that the bad music goes out, as into the garbage can.

"Boyacks decorate like nuts" is kind of a funny one. This goes back to a family identity established by my mother. She loved to decorate, and the holidays provided a wonderful opportunity to do something new with the house. All of her children have carried this on and now it's passing down to our nieces and nephews and the next generations. Really, this family motto was "Brownes decorate like nuts," but we've adopted it as our own. For Christmas, we've amassed forty boxes of decorations, including a nativity set collection of more than 125 nativity sets. (Hah, I caught you. I bet you were just reading that section to your husband saying, "Honey, you thought I was bad—listen to this! This chick has *forty* boxes of Christmas decorations! I don't want to hear any more complaints about my measly ten!" See, I just raised the bar for you. Happy to help promote marital bliss.) The house becomes transformed at Christmas into a fairyland, and the family loves it.

This family motto has brought so much fun into our lives! My kids are totally into it. I knew it was bad when my son on his mission started decorating his little room for each holiday. It has spread! But now the whole neighborhood is into it. They, too, know that Boyacks decorate like nuts. So one time the neighbor kids were over and I had pulled out the Halloween stuff and was absolutely amazed as those children knew where practically every item went. It was as important to them as it was to us, and they looked forward to each holiday as well.

Our stake president's family has an interesting family motto. It's CKATW—Celestial Kingdom All the Way. They use this for a variety of teaching purposes and even have it on their license plates! Of course, they also have a great sense of humor, and Susan likes to joke that some people might say it stands for "Clark Kids Are the Worst!" but I know better. They have raised incredible, faithful children. And much of their success, I believe, stems from this ongoing focus of their whole family identity, which is encapsulated in this motto.

The key to a successful motto is to make it fun and catchy. We could have said, "Boyacks are very reliable people." Snore. . . . "Boyacks don't bail" is much snappier. Make the motto easy to remember and repeat it often at first. Try to use it in fun settings to establish it as a positive thing. When you catch a child doing well, you reinforce with, "Aha! Hendersons are happy campers! I love it when you are cheerful!" What a great reinforcement. That way it doesn't become a stick to beat them over the head with: "Haven't we told you again and again? The early Byrdes get the worm! Why are you late again?" You do not want the child to build a resentment toward the motto or it will be worse than worthless.

Kids are tremendously creative, and coming up with some family mottos can make for a really fun family evening. It's even fun to get the extended family involved. These are great opportunities for creating more "hooks" for teaching principles and independence.

Now let's continue to play *So You Want to Be a PARENT!* (Music.)

Let's play! For 2000 mental sanity points:

You are shopping with your four-year-old. The child begins to have a major temper tantrum—falls to the ground shrieking, kicking, and pounding. What do you do?

a. Walk away calmly and pretend like you don't know the child and mutter under your breath, "I would *never* have a child who did that . . ."

b. Offer the child candy, pop, toys—anything!—if she'll just calm down.

c. Pick up the child and walk out of the store.

d. Begin to cry uncontrollably.

Let's use a lifeline. I'd like to ask the audience. What would you do? Correct answer: "a"! Of course!

All of this parenting must be taken with a sense of humor or you'll never survive. And parenting provides plenty of great chances for some really off-the-wall humor.

Merrilee's Motto: "Money can't buy happiness . . . that's what shopping is for."

Another: "Keep the neighbors guessing."

I was at a lecture and the speaker mentioned a family motto of "All Chairs at the Table," meaning everyone would make it to heaven together. I started giggling uncontrollably as I thought of some new ones: "All monkeys in the cage," "All their marbles in their heads," "All nuts in the candy bar." So enjoy.

Add Family Lore

Family lore is a description of who we are as a family and what we have experienced. It is usually shared in story form and is the essence of family history. What is your family lore?

I've heard some great stories from many families over the years that have become their lore through the telling and retelling over many generations. They can be hilarious and a source of fun for the family. My personal favorite is by my friend whom I shall call Sheila to protect her reputation. Sheila was the bishop's wife and often a bit late to meetings. One week, she ended up having to sit on the front row at church right in front of the bishopric and the visiting stake president. The stake president was quite a . . . how do I say this delicately? A very proper man. (I was going to say a stick-in-the-mud, but that's not really accurate—he was just very formal and proper.) So anyway, she's sitting there and the speaker is speaking and she feels very emotional and reaches in her purse and dabs her face with a tissue many times. Finally she looks down and realizes she's been wiping her face with a minipad!

Needless to say, that story has been told and retold in the family to the delight of them all. What's very funny is Sheila's daughter ended up marrying the stake president's son!! She's hoping he didn't ever notice it, or perhaps he's too polite to say! You might wonder what good a story like that is. It tells volumes about a family with a wonderful sense of humor and a mom who delights in poking fun at herself. What a great gift!

Some family lore stories are serious. My grandfather often told the story of being in World War I. He was in France and was driving a big truck along a road. All of a sudden, the truck just died. He tried and tried to get it restarted, to no avail. Finally, in disgust he climbed out of the truck and walked to the front to see what was going on. As he was walking, he noticed the front tires were up higher than the rear ones. Looking beneath the truck, he realized that it was perched on the edge of a land mine. If he had gone just one inch farther, the truck would have blown up and killed him. He broke out in a sweat and said a quick prayer of thanksgiving. He climbed back in the truck, and it instantly started, and he backed away very carefully. He would always end that story with the comment, "I knew that the Lord had saved my life for some important purpose." Now, what's interesting is that Granddad was not a member of the Church. My dad is a convert. I'm sure Granddad didn't know that his purpose may have been to have a son who would do his temple work for him. *That's* how my dad ends the story when he tells it!

Think of your family lore stories. They often begin with "Remember when . . . ?" and the family will begin to reminisce. Or when grandparents are around—"Did I ever tell you about the time . . ?" These stories are priceless. They can be long or short or funny or sad or meaningful or silly. But they are the story of your family—who you are and what you've experienced.

These stories are priceless teaching tools. You can use them in a variety of settings. "You remind me so much of my grandma. She loved to bake, just like you. Remember the story of how she made the pie from the blueberries by the railroad tracks and won $100 in the state fair and was able to go to college? She was creative in her cooking, just like you." Great teaching moment. You've taught your child to love baking, to love being a homemaker, to be creative in problem-solving, to tap into the creative juices in her brain, the value of college, the love of a cherished grandma, and that the Lord provides answers to prayers in interesting ways—and all in one setting. Whew! That was a power-packed teaching moment!

It's fun to create new family lore. You can recount over and over, "Boy, wasn't that something when Henry won the state championships? There you were, Henry, down four matches with a bum knee. And in you went like a terror, winning the next five. It was incredible. Sarah, remember the look on his face when he hopped around with the trophy? It was incredible." What fabulous new family lore you're creating. The powerful story of "Henry the Underdog Triumphs."

So you're working on The Plan, and you're sharing stories of Great Uncle Otis and the Model T. You're teaching about making the bed, and little Jason starts laughing and says, "Remember Grandpa Edward telling us about getting squished when the bunk bed collapsed?"

All of these things—establishing a family identity, developing family mottos, and sharing family lore—are incredibly important teaching tools in raising independent kids.

Using all of these methods gives your family tremendous focus and sets a tone for where the family is headed. They are great tools for setting goals for the family in a rather subtle and yet very positive way. You could use "Taylors are team players" even though the Taylors currently would like to kill each other most of the time. The kids may not realize that you chose that motto to build family unity while you were working on getting to cooperation and teamwork.

Establishing a family identity is also very liberating. You can identify the strengths and positives of your own family and let go of a lot of guilt. You can beat yourself up thinking, "Gee, we should be wearing matching outfits like the Griswolds and going to Disney World every year." Or you can relax and realize, "Hey, our family is the camping and do-your-own-wash type of family!" See how liberating that is? You can let go of other family identities and hang on to your own. Frankly, neither one is better or worse—they're just a means to the end of raising children. (No—I was wrong. The second one is definitely better!)

Finally, using these tools gives children security and identity.

They can say, "I know who a Garcia is." Do you remember the end of the story of Stuart Little, the mouse adopted by a human family? At the end he says, "I'm a Little! I'm Stuart Little. I'm STUART LITTLE! . . . Every Little knows how to find a Little House." That speaks volumes. He felt a unity and bond with his family and understood what it meant to be in a family that loved him. Our children will know who and what they are, and that sense of unity in a family is invaluable.

One year I wrote a poem for my parents and my in-laws, kind of in Dr. Seuss style, and I kept it for my children so they would know who they are:

What Is a Boyack?

I have surveyed Boyacks far and wide
And discovered to my surprise
That they're a lot alike in many ways
More than noses, hair, or eyes.

So what is a Boyack, you may ask,
And just what makes them unique?
Well the answers are quite simple,
At my list you may take a peek.

A Boyack is very generous
With treats and gifts galore,
But frankly the grandkids are spoiled
And the grandparents just pile on more!

A Boyack can work very hard
And stay 'til the task is done.
They're very handy to have around
To make the work seem fun.

Now this you must also know—
All Boyacks love to eat sweets.

They love ice cream and cookies
And pop and all other treats.

A Boyack loves to shop
To go both morning and night
And loves to be in fashion
And dress themselves just right.

Now Boyack girls love crafts,
Their creativity never fails;
But Boyack boys are adventurous
On bikes or mountains or trails.

Sundays are special to Boyacks,
As their families gather round,
To talk of things that matter
And pass the popcorn 'round!

And this is also true:
A Boyack saves and saves,
Whether books and tapes or clothes
They've got it for rainy days!

Boyacks make the cutest babies,
Chubby towheads all around,
And everyone dotes on the youngest
But plenty of love abounds.

A Boyack has great faith
And loves our Savior true,
And tries their best to do what's right
And be good neighbors too.

But most of all Boyacks have one thing
More important than the rest,
A Boyack has love for all other Boyacks
And feels all Boyacks are best.

An important part of training independent children is to give children security and identity and a firm base from which to grow. Their heritage is a precious gift, and as you use those lessons you have learned to raise them well, the legacy of their ancestors can be a blessing to them.

Family Environment

One of my favorite methods for training children is through the use of "silent teaching." This can be an incredibly effective method. I'm sure you're curious to know what it means. Silent teaching is teaching that goes on without the lectures, without the actions, without anything overt.

One fantastic way in which silent teaching is imparted is through the family environment. You've probably heard the story told by Spencer W. Kimball of a woman whose sons all went to sea and took jobs that involved the ocean. The mother was at a loss to explain it, but President Kimball couldn't help but notice the huge picture of the ocean over the living-room couch. He spoke about silent teaching and encouraged us as LDS families to put up pictures of the temple in our homes.

The home environment is a vastly underused resource. Try to spend some time sitting in the various rooms of your home, and ask yourself in each case, "What do I feel in this room? What do I find myself thinking of in this room?" Ponder each room with these questions in mind. Then ask, "How could I use this room to teach my children?" I'll share a few ideas that I've seen used, but don't limit yourself to these.

Family pictures

First, of course, is the "humungous family picture." This is important and worth the investment. I think a family portrait speaks volumes about who the family is. It is a defining statement of the home. There are ways to have this done less expensively, and even a medium-sized picture with nice matting makes a definitive statement. Think of the message and the feelings that it conveys: "You are part of something big." "You are loved." "You are a part of us and we're all a team." Crucial teaching.

An extension of this is the "family pictures wall." My sister Linda loved photography, and when she got married, she began decorating a large wall in her family room with family pictures: photos of their son, their family, her parents and family, her husband's parents and family, and on and on. I always absolutely loved that wall, so the minute I got married, I began my own. We have a large wall now with all kinds of pictures. My mother-in-law loved it and has begun a huge wall of *her* own. We have a great picture of my husband in a lake in Chile ready to baptize someone, and one of him entering the Missionary Training Center. There's a shot of one of our sons at age eight next to a picture of my husband at age eight, and it's frightening how much they look alike! There are pictures of grandparents long since passed on. There are pictures of our family in rather silly locations doing silly things. There are pictures of me and my hubby when we were children. Our wall has grown and grown.

What does this wall teach? "Here is the history of our family and of you, our child." One day my son asked what would happen if he died before me. I walked him and his brothers all over to the wall and pointed to their great-grandparents and said, "See these people? [And I described each of them.] They will greet you when you pass on. They'll be right there to give you giant hugs and kisses and they'll be so excited to see you. And if Daddy and I die before you, we'll be right there with them to hug and kiss you." The children were filled with peace. This wall teaches them about love as you talk about how these people feel about them. It teaches them goals. (See Brother on his mission? See Aunt and Uncle getting married in the temple?) It teaches them about eternity. The lessons are endless.

Another twist is using family pictures in a creative way. I decorated my living room with a giant picture of a close-up of the hands of God and Adam from the mural of the Sistine Chapel. It's very inspiring. I put it there because I meet with clients in my living room, and when they ask about it, it gives me a chance to talk to them about the Creation or the priesthood or the plan of salvation or whatever I feel prompted to say. Talk about stealth teaching! Ha! So anyway, I was searching for an idea to use in the entryway to continue with the theme of "hands." So I took black-and-white close-up photos of my family members' hands doing what they love. We have Great-Grandpa Poulsen's gnarled hands strumming his old guitar. There are Parker's smooth young hands playing the piano, and Connor's wiry hands on the computer. There's a shot of Grandma and Granddad Browne holding hands with their wrinkled, beautiful hands that have been together sixty years. It's incredible. Every single person who walks in our home is awestruck and asks what it means. The children or I explain whose hands are in each picture and what they're doing.

The possibilities for using family pictures are endless. I'm dying to do feet pictures in the bathroom! (In the kids' bathroom I did have them put giant handprints in all the primary colors all over the walls. It's adorable!)

Family banner

Another idea is the family banner. My sister Kathe (aka "Fabulous Mom") had her family do a banner for family home evening many, many years ago. She gathered supplies such as felt and markers and prepared a large fabric banner before the night. Then they talked about who the family was and had the various family members make items to add to the banner. So there's a temple where they began the marriage. There's a hand to symbolize helping hands. There's a beehive for hard work. There's a house with lit windows and a happy face on it to symbolize their happy home. There's also smoke coming out of the chimney in the shape of an infinity sign up to the sun, symbolizing that their family is eternal and heading to the celestial kingdom. Also, they put on a snowflake to signify that they are each individuals, and finally a Book of Mormon because they read their scriptures. This has hung in their home for decades and is a simple visual reminder about what is important to them. It teaches many things to the children who see it day after day after day.

Family glory wall

One idea I love is the family glory wall. I've seen these in many homes. Some families have their children's artwork framed beautifully and displayed on a wall. Others have a glory mantel with their kids' trophies displayed. We, of course, have a Scout wall with all our boys' Eagle plaques and Arrow of Light plaques. We have Scout pictures and other Scout memorabilia. On another wall, Steve mounted all the boys' Pinewood Derby cars in order and had small brass plaques etched with their name

and year. There sit those twelve cars way up high, a hilarious commentary on our family. The first few cars are frighteningly homely, and those last ones are really sleek. We all get a chuckle out of that.

So what could you display on your family glory wall? It could have items made by the kids, awards, their artwork, Dad's sculpture that won at the fair, Mom's blue ribbon, the kids' certificates, whatever. Make sure it is nice and not just a sloppy clump of items stabbed up on the wall. You want this to be a source of pride and joy for the family. One day I was trying to fill a wall space and grabbed an old chalk drawing my son had done. It was actually very good. I put it in a really nice frame I had with a gorgeous matte job left over from some other project, and it looked stunning. I asked a friend how much she thought I had to pay for that original artwork, and she estimated $500. I got a good laugh out of that. Do you know how it makes my son feel to see his artwork displayed so beautifully?

The lessons of the family glory wall range from striving for excellence to learning that we all have gifts. They add to family unity. They teach love and approval and confidence. Again, the lessons are innumerable.

And don't forget to include Mom and Dad in these things. Those displays are incredible silent teachers. They say, "See what Mom did?" or "See how Dad did exactly what we're teaching you to do?" The kids will have tremendous respect for you when they see what you, too, have done.

One of my favorite quotes regarding children is, "Children have never been very good at listening to their elders, but they have never failed to imitate them" (James Baldwin). That quote speaks volumes. Our children will always imitate us. (How many times have you caught yourself saying, "I sound just like my mother!") So *use* that imitation. Foster it. Show all the good things in Mom and Dad that you want your children to emulate. It is powerful teaching.

Other visual reminders

Never underestimate the power of the family environment. Put up pictures of the Savior, pictures of the temple, pictures of the prophet. Put up quotes you like. I have one in Hebrew carved in stone that was in my home growing up. From time to time the kids ask to be reminded what it says. (It's in *Hebrew*, remember?) It says, "In a place where there are no men, strive to be a man." I have pillows with great quotes on them. The house is loaded with stuff, and it's all so subtle that the kids have no idea what's going on!

In friends' homes I have seen framed copies of "The Family: A Proclamation to the World," statues of pioneers or Church leaders or the Savior, framed quotes such as "Return with Honor," and more. We all just smile and say, "Yes, that sounds like a Mormon home." I say it's more—it's a *teaching* home. Children seeing these images and words will have lessons reinforced day after day after day. One of my friends has rocks etched with important quotes. Another has cute knick-knacks that have cute sayings as well. In the hall of our boys' rooms, we put up a giant orange sign that says, "Missionary Construction Zone." I could go on for hours. These things all teach lessons. And the important part is—you didn't have to say a word!

So go through your whole house with the eye of a teaching parent. Don't go crazy and stick quotes in every room! Be selective. But think creatively about what more you could do. Another tip is to move things around. If things stay in the same place, they can become just part of the wallpaper, and the kids tune them out somewhat. So add new pictures; move the pillow. Point things out to the kids and then let them learn.

Family history mementoes

Another way to use the visual environment is for lessons on family history. Display Grandpa's hat in the corner. Put up Aunt Betty's painting on the wall. Set Great-Grandma's wooden spoon on the mantel. These objects are incredible, physical reminders of who went before us and that they were real people. Don't just keep these things safely stored away. Put them out where they can become part of the family's experience. Tell the story to the kids of how Aunt Betty started painting. Tell them about how Great-Grandma baked bread in Germany to save money to come to America. And have them really touch those things and see them in your home.

Music

Another part of the family environment is music. Don't underestimate the power of this resource! You've heard this a ton, so I just want to mention it here briefly as a reminder to add it into your analysis of how you can use your family environment to teach and train. Music is powerful for inspiring our kids. And here again, they don't realize what they're learning. Every Sunday, I turn on the Mormon Tabernacle Choir. One particular CD, the one with the Broadway hits, has about gotten worn right through because I find it so inspirational. When I hear, "To Dream the Impossible Dream," I get a huge lump in my throat and want to go conquer the world. Anyway, the teenage kids would always gripe about it, particularly my oldest son, who is a big music buff. Sunday after Sunday, I would put it on and he would complain.

One day I ran across a paper this boy had written in his senior year of high school about the influence music had in his life. I was surprised to run across this paragraph: "I really love the music of the Mormon Tabernacle Choir and find it truly inspiring. My mother would always make us listen to it every Sunday morning and I loved how it made me feel. Now I know all the words and they run through my head. It is great." Okay, so knock me over with a feather! I'm thinking, "Who is this kid?" We have no idea how much influence that music can have—much more than we realize.

Using these principles helps bring the Spirit into your home in a powerful way. Then the standard becomes, "We will allow into our home only those things that invite the Spirit." And the children know that if anyone brings in bad videos or music or clothing or books, *they go in the trash*. Why? "Because that does not allow the Spirit to be in our home." We use this principle a lot in our family, and it's the *principle* that controls our home environment rather than the parents saying, "I hate that stuff," or, "That's trash." We just rely on, "We want the Spirit to be in our home. When this is here, it can't be." Then that decision becomes a positive affirmation of what we want our home to be. It's hard for the kids to argue with that one—although they'll try . . .

Develop a Family Timeline

A helpful tool for organizing your family and The Plan is to develop a family timeline. My sister developed this idea and, of course, I stole it. Frankly, everyone needs a sister who is ten years older to get great ideas from!

Here's how it works. You gather the whole family together, bribe them with food if you have to, and have either a big chalkboard or a large pad of paper handy. Announce that you're going to work on a family timeline. The whole family will gasp with joy and congratulate you on having such a brilliant idea and will enthusiastically participate.

Okay, that's the theory, anyway. In my family, it worked more like this: I announced that for family home evening, we

145

were going to do this family timeline. Immediately everyone, including my usually supportive spouse, began to grumble and complain. A large fight erupted (lovingly referred to as the activity portion of our home evening), and it got so bad that Daddy closed the evening. So they all started doing their own things: two were playing a game, Dad was reattached to his computer, the others were just poking each other, and I sat there with my pad of paper. Undeterred, I might add.

So I began filling in years and names and activities. I would talk out loud to myself, "Let's see, if Parker is fourteen, he should be about to be a Life Scout and in the ninth grade . . . and Tanner should be a Star Scout, and . . ." Tanner popped up his head and said, "Hey, I'm gonna be a Life Scout at the same time as Parker!" Parker argued, "No you won't." I stopped what I was doing and said, "Okay, well, each of you figure out at what age you'll be what, and I'll stick it in." I ignored them as they started negotiating, like it was some big peace accord or something. They then informed me of what ages they would be achieving what, and I dutifully plugged it in.

I then called out to my husband, "Where do you want to go on our family vacation next year?" He said, "I was thinking of doing a Southwest thing like around Mesa Verde and that area." "That sounds cool," said one of the boys, "We studied that in school." So I plugged it in.

Well, you can guess, after about fifteen minutes, the whole family was over there right by me putting in their two cents' worth on what year to put each activity of their lives. It was hilarious. It's at times like these that a mom just bites her tongue and smiles at her "cooperative" family. My tongue has a huge scar, did I mention that?

Anyway, to do a family timeline, you put down a bunch of years (at least ten) and then put in the names of the family members and what they'll want to do that year. I also put in family vacations because we have a plan to make sure our kids see all the places we want them to see by the time they grow up. Here is an example of a few years for our family:

1999

Steve	Lose weight, run 500 miles, organize office
Merr	Lose weight, read NT, D&C, B of M, P of G P
Connor	Graduate high school, work summer, BYU
Brennan	7th/8th grade, Life Scout, Eagle Scout Project
Parker	4th/5th grade, band, Arrow of Light, Nov.—Boy Scouts
Tanner	2nd/3rd grade, Cub Scouts—Wolf, Baptism!
Summer Vacation	Redwoods/California
Other Vacation	Spring skiing in Utah

2000

Steve	Keep job!
Merr	Marriage Initiative, Proposition 22 Area Leader
Connor	BYU, work summer, Elder
Brennan	8th/9th grade, seminary, Teacher
Parker	5th/6th grade, band, First Class Scout, Deacon
Tanner	3rd/4th grade, Bear Scout, Faith in God
Summer Vacation	Yellowstone
Other Vacation	Spring skiing in Utah

2001

Steve	Organize family videos, learn iMovie, BSA advancement chairman
Merr	Work on new lectures, do Nativity Open House
Connor	Mission
Brennan	9th/10th grade, On My Honor, seminary
Parker	6th/7th grade, Life Scout
Tanner	4th/5th grade, Webelos Scout, Gospel in Action, band

| Summer Vacation | Canada |
| Other Vacation | Spring skiing in Utah |

2002

Steve	Digitize 500 35mm slides, run 500 miles
Merr	Write book, teach seminary, run for Central Committee
Connor	Mission
Brennan	10th/11th grade, seminary, Eagle Scout, Priest, get a job
Parker	7th/8th grade, Teacher
Tanner	5th/6th grade, Arrow of Light, Boy Scout
Summer Vacation	Indian ruins, Arizona, Utah

This is just a short version. I've left out the more personal goals.

Now let's talk about how to use this tool to raise independent youngsters. This is a great planning tool for the family. You see, ah, we'll have three boys in school at BYU at once (hopefully!), and maybe we should buy a condo for them. So we need to start saving for that five years in advance. Let's plug that in. This year we'll have a boy going to the temple for the first time, so let's do family home evenings on the temple. Let's plan a trip doing the Church history tour for when the oldest is home from a mission and get the other kids to start reading *The Work and the Glory* to get them excited.

You can see the whole family's life summarized in a few pages and can begin to plan and plug in certain events and activities and accomplishments you want to do. It allows you to start teaching and training in advance and to gear the family's plan around preparing the children for those items.

Also, the timeline recommits the family to the goals of each member. There's nothing like seeing in black-and-white print: "Mission," "College," or "Eagle Scout" to reinforce those goals and make them seem almost an eventuality. Also, you can see what the family needs to do as a whole to prepare to get each person where he or she wants to be. This is also a flexible, constantly changing tool.

Family Goals—Where Are We Going As a Family?

Welcome back to *So You Want to Be a PARENT!* (Music.)

Let's play! For 30,000 mental sanity points:

You come home one day to find that your second son is sporting neon-yellow hair. As you comment on his new and unique coif, he tells you that his older brother did it for him. You now have visions of him passing the sacrament in neon hair. What do you do?

a. Insist that the child be shaved bald immediately.

b. Impose the parental curse on older brother.

c. Ignore it completely, and when people ask what happened to your son's hair, comment, "His older brother happened."

d. Begin to cry uncontrollably.

Remember General Patton's battle cry: "Pick your battles!" (By the way, we picked "c.")

We have to pick our priorities, whether we're talking about rules we insist be followed or goals we want to work on. If we don't have priorities as a family, we are like a rudderless boat going nowhere.

Effective families and outstanding children don't "just happen." They are the result of planning and organization. And all of that requires setting family goals. You may be surprised that I left this for last, but this is why I did: By now, your brain has been chewing a bit on how to administer The Plan and is filled with tools and ideas on how to do that. So now that you have some of the skills, tools, and elements in place, it's the perfect time to step back and look at the big picture.

Setting family goals is a completely worthless task . . . unless you are willing to actually think about them and write them down. If you are just going to blab, blab, blab and say, "We should do this . . ." or "We should do that . . ." or "I feel so guilty that we're not doing this or that . . . ," stop now and save yourself some much-needed oxygen. Setting goals is a serious task. It requires commitment and follow-through. Those are the hard parts.

There are many areas in which the family can set goals. *Never* try to cover all of these in one family meeting. Your family will blow up! Fit them in occasionally and in small chunks.

1. Religious goals

In our culture, these are somewhat no-brainers. Tons has been and will be written about them, so I will just cover them briefly: daily family prayer, weekly family home evening, family scripture study. The top three. If you do nothing else, set these goals, commit to them, and follow through. How many parents do you know who complain that their kids are giving them fits, but when you ask if they are doing these three things, most of them are not? The prophets and apostles have told us over and over and *over* and OVER to do these things and we will be blessed. My opinion is that if we are not doing these things, we can't whine and complain that we're not getting the help we need from the Lord to raise our kids. We need to *start with His plan first*. Then He will bless us with the rest.

Other religious goals will include participating in religious awards programs such as Faith in God, Duty to God, Young Women Personal Progress, attendance at church meetings, going to the temple, serving missions, and so on. You can add in family study goals such as reading from the standard works or reading religious books.

2. Financial goals

It takes just one quick look at the family timeline to make you realize that Amy needs to be saving for college by a certain year and Alan needs to have his mission savings completed. You can plan for those wonderful weddings and other expenses. Setting financial goals and discussing them as a family can help tremendously with buy-in—not to mention its effectiveness in teaching your children how to budget and save and plan for the future.

You can explain that you need money for your retirement and talk about your commitment to that. It's interesting that kids just perceive you as this big money machine and don't realize your commitments to other financial obligations. Giving them a rundown on retirement savings is great. One of my kids said, "You don't need to save for retirement." I answered, "Great! So we're moving in with you and your wife and you're paying for everything! Yahoo!" He quickly reevaluated, deciding that our saving for retirement wasn't such a bad idea after all.

Often, parents limit these conversations to just themselves. It's so valuable to set these financial goals as a family, with the kids having input and understanding. For example, you could sit as a family and say, "We need to redecorate the kitchen. What should we do and how can we save to get there?" Involve them in the process.

3. Recreational goals

I love President Hinckley's counsel on the importance of the family playing together. He and his wife are marvelous examples of parents who have raised their children with joy and fun. Another area in which to make goals as a family is the area of recreation.

Is your family going to participate in sports? Which ones and when? Do you need classes or equipment? I remember one year my dad (who, now that I look back, may have been in a slight midlife crisis) suggested that we take up snow skiing as a family sport. We all discussed it and (bless my mother) got the equipment and took classes and we've been a skiing family ever since. At the time, Mom and Dad were in their mid-forties and had never skied in their lives. What a credit to both of them!

So I have to share with you a story about Mom and skiing. Here she is about forty-five, and the family decides to take up a new sport. Mom is game—which is pretty surprising because Mom's not a real physical-type person. So anyway, after we've been skiing for a couple of years, Mom is still struggling to get the hang of it. One day we're skiing at Caberfe in the middle of Michigan. (I grew up in Detroit.) My brother and I are going up the rope tow. (Ick, skiing in Michigan meant lots of rope tows where that long, running rope takes you up the hill.)

Up ahead is Mom. Now about halfway up the rope tow some accident strikes. I think Mom let the rope drop and then picked it up again, after having gotten it between her legs. Anyway, we look up in horror to see my mother going up the hill backwards with the rope tow between her legs. Disaster is about to occur because at the end of the rope tow, the rope goes way up about eight feet high to hit the pulley and return over the skiers' heads back down the hill. So we're watching Mom about to be severed in a most painful way, and we're screaming, "Mom, let go of the rope! Let *go* of the rope!" Finally, Mom comes to her senses and drops the rope and falls. The entire line of skiers breathes a sigh of relief.

It was shortly after that that my mother ceased participating in an active way in the family sport. She became the coach on the sidelines who dressed us, fed us, praised us, and safely read a book in the lodge during runs. I think it was the nightmare of envisioning her whole life as a split personality that did her in!

Is your family going to go on vacations? Where and when?

Usually, families who don't plan, don't go. It's often not the lack of money but lack of planning that can kill a family vacation. Vacations are such fabulous opportunities for your family! They can be done incredibly cheaply if you're willing to camp. My parents took us to Europe where we camped for about two dollars a night! It just takes some creativity.

4. Behavioral goals

We're all familiar with these goals that our families work on constantly. You may be working on contention (eliminating it or perfecting it?), honesty, selfless service, or others. Usually we work on our behavior for a little while and then let it drop.

Remember two principles here: One is the Bit-by-Bit Principle, which we've already discussed. The other principle is this: Every little bit makes a difference. Sometimes we feel unsuccessful, thinking, "Man, we worked on that honesty thing for a whole six months and here we are three years later and it's creeping up again. We're failures!" Not so. We raise children and change behavior bit by bit. They learn about honesty at age four. Then again at eight and maybe repeat at twelve and again at sixteen and on and on you go. Each time they learn it differently. And bit by bit you end up with an honest child.

Bottom line, every little bit makes a difference. So you worked on eliminating contention in the home for a few months and then fizzled out. Even working on it for that short while made a contribution and improvement to your family. It helped bring the Spirit into your home. It made each of you a little bit better. Every tiny little bit of effort you make in raising excellent children is important and will make a difference in the whole. And you will be shocked when they come back years later and mention the most inconsequential thing that made a huge difference in their lives. Just keep plugging away at those little bits.

As I mentioned before, the key with all the goals is in writing them down and committing to them. My kids are very familiar with what we call the 3 Percent Rule. One day my dad told us the story of a study done at Harvard Business School. They tracked a graduating class and found that 3 percent actually wrote down their career goals. In ten years, that 3 percent of graduates were making more than the other 97 percent combined. I'm not sure if it's true, but it was a big hit with my kids!

After setting the family goals (which can change from year to year), it's helpful to then distill this thinking down to each child and help them set their own personal goals. Every year, on Christmas night, we sit as a family and talk about the Savior. We then each decide on one "gift" we will give to the Savior for the coming year. We write these down on white slips of paper and put them into a small, white stocking that hangs on our mantel in the living room all year long. (I "borrowed" this idea from my great friend Susan Clark.) Throughout the year, the kids see that stocking and remember their gifts, which we discuss from time to time throughout the year. It may be "Pray every day" or "Be kinder to my brothers" or "Attend the temple weekly" or whatever. At the end of the year, we talk about how we did and set new goals.

Another way to help kids set goals is one I read about in the *Church News,* I think. Each year the kids set their own goals, such as "Get all A's and B's in school," "Get my Duty to God award for deacon," "Be completely honest at home," or whatever they want. And yes, you'll have one child who will want to list ten goals and one who wants only one or, preferably, none. So we settle for about half a dozen and print them off the computer in big, nice print onto really nice paper. Then I put each child's goals into an 8x10 picture frame and hang them on the wall right by their beds. They see this all the time, and it has been very, very motivational.

We also have *huge* white boards in the kids' rooms that cover most of one wall. This board is absolutely *the* most important item in each boy's room. They list their goals on there all the time, including short-term goals like, "Clean out the hamster cage." It is a very flexible reminder board and they use it constantly.

Let's take a break to keep playing *So You Want to Be a PARENT!* (Music.)

You're all doing very well. For 400,000 mental sanity points, answer the following:

You had a twenty-dollar bill that you left on your dresser. It is now missing. You line up all the children and ask who took it. All of them insist, "I didn't take it!" What do you do?

a. Apologize profusely to all of them for accusing them unfairly.

b. Dock them all an allowance to pay it back.

c. Hold a garage sale of your children's belongings.

d. Begin to cry uncontrollably.

Mrs. Pythagorean's Theorem: All three corners of a triangle are responsible for the interior of the triangle. In other words, holding everyone responsible will usually cause a huge fight that will eventually result in the culprit being identified. Or sometimes not . . . but I'd choose "b" anyway.

Setting goals in family planning meetings involves the whole family, so all will have equal responsibility and (somewhat) equal commitment. Again, reevaluate throughout the year to see if you're on track and to see if the goal is still relevant to the family.

Helping the children and the family set and accomplish goals is pivotal to raising truly independent kids who are equipped with a strength and skill that will last them a lifetime. The actual "doing" of the agreed-upon goal is the most important part, and that kind of training, day after day, year after year, is tremendous in its impact. The difference in adulthood between those who learned how to set and accomplish goals and those who didn't is glaring, as I'm sure you've noticed.

All of the ideas discussed in this chapter provide focus for the family. Now you have a focused family, and that's incredible. The family and all its members have direction; they're not wandering aimlessly waiting for time to just go by and the kids to just get bigger. The tools are available—so use them!

Now for our final question on *So You Want to Be a PARENT!* (Music.)

For one million mental sanity points, answer this!

You are listening to a talk extolling children, and just as the speaker says, "Blessed are the children!" you realize that the child on your left has the child on your right in a headlock and they are trying to kill each other in your lap and you're sitting right in front of the speaker. What do you do?

a. Join them in the free-for-all and work out some of your pent-up aggression.

b. Lift them both and carry them down the aisle to the foyer.

c. Clamp your hands over their mouths so they don't make noise and keep nodding at the speaker in total agreement.

d. Begin to cry uncontrollably.

Brother Murphy's Law: Anything bad can and will happen in church.

After all is said and done, hang in there and keep that grin on your face!

CHAPTER 8

How to Help Kids with Emotional and Spiritual Development

A lot of issues revolve around the emotions of parenting. Let's face it: Parenting today is much more intense than it was in our parents' generation. My older friend Joan commented on this one day. "In my day," she said, "we just said hello to the kids when they came home from school, and they would run out and play until dark. We never worried where they were or who they were with. They were just out playing. Now all my kids have to keep such close track of their children to keep them safe. It's a lot harder now."

A big part of this is that Satan is having a field day going after our kids. The media doesn't help much. You could drive yourself into a terrified frenzy just from reading in the newspaper what is happening to children every day. And the risks that families confront today are much higher. Our kids face the evil of the world head-on and much earlier than we ever did: immorality, drugs, filthy language, sexuality, materialism, homosexuality, deviancy, violence, and the list could go on and on. All of this is splashed everywhere and often is packaged to look appealing and desirable.

In a letter dated 11 February 1999, signed by the First Presidency of the Church, Gordon B. Hinckley, Thomas S.

Monson, and James E. Faust described what parents must do: "We call upon parents to devote their best efforts to the teaching and rearing of their children in gospel principles which will keep them close to the Church. The home is the basis of a righteous life, and no other instrumentality can take its place or fulfill its essential functions in carrying forward this God-given responsibility.

"We counsel parents and children to give highest priority to family prayer, family home evening, gospel study and instruction, and wholesome family activities. However worthy and appropriate other demands or activities may be, they must not be permitted to displace the divinely appointed duties that only parents and families can adequately perform" ("Policies, Announcements, and Appointments," *Ensign,* June 1999, 80).

Never before in the history of our world has quality parenting on emotional and spiritual issues been more necessary. The *only* way our children are going to make it through is if they have deep roots of faith, testimony, and emotional strength.

Given this backdrop of the world we live in, I thought I'd take some time to discuss some ideas relative to dealing with emotional and spiritual issues. Hopefully, they will help.

How to Talk to Kids and Have Them Hear You

It's not enough for us to blah, blah, blah to our kids day in and day out. They need to *hear* us. This is something we all struggle with, and I think it's particularly true of moms. Sometimes we feel like if we can throw enough words at our kids, some will stick. Recently, my son turned to me and said, "Do your lips ever stop flapping?" I stopped my yammering and burst out laughing. I said, "Well, no, they don't! So get used to it!" But it was a valuable lesson that I have learned and need to relearn a zillion times.

When to talk

I've read many Church articles that strongly push the idea of holding formal interviews with children. Other articles talk about structured time talking to kids. These are good ideas, but we need to adjust them to fit the needs of our individual families. Knowing when and how to talk to kids will increase our effectiveness dramatically.

We have formal times in talking to our kids and informal times. These will vary depending on the child and depending on the age. Having a formal, lengthy conversation with a three-year-old for longer than two or three minutes is rather silly, for example, but you'll have lots of informal interactions while rocking in a chair, reading a book, and driving in the car.

Some kids love to schedule a big, structured talk with Dad. Others will clamp their mouths shut and dare Dad to get something out of them. Don't feel bad if one way of communicating doesn't work. The key is to communicate, and that can be done on a ski slope, in the kitchen, or wherever.

This is so true when it's time to discuss human intimacy—the famous "birds and bees" talk. With a couple of our kids, we set up a formal discussion with books and pictures. When we tried this with another of our children (we were still young and learning), he promptly crammed his fingers in his ears and made loud noises with his mouth, "BLA-BLA-BLA!" until we gave up and walked away. In fact, it has taken about six years to get the whole discussion done with that child in tiny bits and pieces—*very* informally—because if he gets a whiff of the topic, in go the fingers into the ears.

Some topics lend themselves to informal discussions and lots of listening. Remember to focus on what works for each child at his or her age and level of maturity. And remember that what is "appropriate" will be different for each child and each age.

"Talking time"

Another important communication strategy is to figure out when your child's "talking time" is. You know what I mean: Some kids are wonderful in the morning—cooperative, happy, and willing to listen. Others are in a coma or at best in a grunting, monosyllabic mode. Those children, the night owls, usually warm up in the evening. Figuring out how your child is hardwired will help you be much more successful. When you need to discuss something important or want to connect, time it to when the child is the most receptive.

Now, sometimes this will be in conflict with the parent's own internal clock. I am definitely a morning person, and my hubby is definitely a night owl. If I know something needs to be discussed with our night-owl child, I'll often ask my husband to handle it because he's more alert and attentive at that hour. I, on the other hand, would be short-tempered, impatient, and exhausted. Why fight rhythms? The minute I start trying to talk to my night-owl child in the morning, I have to stop myself and think, "This isn't going to work! It'll have to wait." You want to be successful, right? Timing is everything.

This is particularly true with teenagers, who are often in their night-owl mode. Sitting on the edge of their bed in the evenings to talk will make for conversations that are much more relaxed and not as likely to trigger an emotional storm. The best times my husband has communicating with our teenage sons are after 11 P.M. Luckily, one of us is a night owl! I'm certainly not.

When your child first comes home from school is often a terrible time to have a lengthy chat. Most kids are tired and hungry. Give them some time to decompress, eat, and relax before you tackle big discussions. One of my kids was so wound up from being at school, he would come home and kick the couch for twenty minutes. You think I'm exaggerating? I'm not! I purposely hung out in my room for a while until he could wind down a bit. If I was even around, he would blow up. But if I waited for about twenty minutes, he was much, much better and we could have a nice chat.

Don't open a shaken can

Picture this: You have just taken two cans of soda out of the fridge. You set the first one down carefully on the counter. The second one, you shake up for a good thirty seconds before setting it down. Now: Which one do you want to open? The settled one, I would assume, unless you're really in the mood for a soda shower.

Many parents make the mistake of trying to talk to their children when either they or their children are upset. I've heard some pretty funny stories of how these discussions go. My friend Dennis was chewing out his son for playing with the ball inside the house. He got more and more upset and finally said, "I *mean* it! Quit playing with this ball in the house!" and threw the ball down hard . . . and it bounced up and broke something. Needless to say, the whole family busted a gut laughing and the children tease their dad to this day about it.

If emotions are escalating, stop yourself. It doesn't matter if it's you or your child who is getting heated up. Just stop and say, "We are really upset about this now. Let's wait and discuss this later." You are not being wishy-washy—you are in *control*. We all know that things are best discussed with cooler heads. So be the adult, be in control, and pick a better time to talk about it.

Taking a break will allow many things to happen. It will allow both of you to have a bit more perspective. It's less likely that anger will take over what is really being felt. You'll both be more communicative. It's hard to do, but a great practice to put into place.

Be flexible with age changes

I hear it all the time: "He used to talk to me all the time and now he won't say a thing." "She talks to her friends but she won't talk to me." "Will our relationship ever be the way it was? They seem to hate me so much."

Don't worry too much. The child who could not stop talking at age seven may become mute at fourteen. Children change all the time, and we need to be flexible with their changing desires to talk. Allow them to take the lead, at least somewhat. And keep trying. But be reassured that if you had a good relationship with the child before fourteen, and you keep trying gently, it will usually resurface at about seventeen or eighteen. Complaining, "You don't talk to me anymore," will do absolutely no good. If they have a topic they're warmed up about, go there and let them stay there.

One of my sons loves motorcycles. I happened to start driving one at age forty. (I know, I know. In fact, I was talking about this at an Education Week lecture and one of the participants came up to my mother-in-law afterward and said, "That whole motorcycle thing is a metaphor, right?" My mother-in-law assured him that I really had a shiny, red motorcycle. My mother still wonders where she went wrong.) Anyway, this son likes bikes. So we talk bikes. Another son likes cars, so we talk cars. Another son likes computers, so we talk computers. Actually, most of the time my son talks about his passion and I make appropriate comments like, "Now *that's* a sweet ride!" (motorcycle talk) or, "I don't get it" (computer stuff), and he explains.

If you can keep that level of conversation going and avoid the temptation to stick in stuff you really want to discuss with them, your relationship has a good chance of surviving.

The same goes with little ones. Let them talk and talk about their friends, their teachers, their toys. Have lots and lots of those conversations without any hint of things you want them to improve on. Bite your tongue. Go ahead, it's good to start this habit early.

Treating the kids fairly

Parents often worry about damaging their children's self-esteem, and one of the biggest complaints or worries is whether they're treating their children "fairly." Now, this is the number-one tool in the "Kids' Arsenal of Guilt Trips." All children were born with this arsenal. So your child will often whip out her favorite tool and howl, "But that's not FAAAAAAAIIIIIIRRRR!"

Let me share with you a little story told by actress Marlo Thomas. Some dedicated, wonderful parents had a son and named him Ralph. Then they had another child and decided that they had to be absolutely fair, so they named her Ralph. Then they had a third baby and named her Ralph too—just to be fair. They wanted to be fair to all their children, so when it was time for one child to do homework, they made them all do it—dumping books in the baby's crib. All the kids had to wear diapers, because that was fair. All the kids had to take long naps, just to be fair. All had to wear braces to be completely fair to all.

Time goes on, and of course the kids are complaining. The parents say, "Where did we go wrong? We treated you exactly the same! Isn't that fair?" The children said they didn't *want* to be treated fairly and that maybe, once in a while, the parents could treat them differently.

I love that story because it shows how absurd it is to try to treat our children absolutely "fairly" (or the same) all the time.

Frankly, I think the best answer to, "It's not FAAAAAAIIIIIR-RRRR!" is to say, "Yup, you're right. It's not fair." And to get on with it. Of course, they will howl with protest. Oh, well.

Most parents do a very good job of treating their children equitably. Occasionally we will treat one child differently from the others, but there is usually a good reason for that: financial issues, personality issues, time issues, or whatever.

We need to not get hooked into this argument. Just refuse to go there. Say, "Well, life is not fair. That's that." Don't argue, don't explain. Because to a child, "fair" is really them getting their way. So don't succumb to this complaint. It will never make any difference and the self-inflicted guilt will chew you up.

Don't try to explain

Tool number two in the "Kids' Arsenal of Guilt Trips" is "But *why?*" This seems like a reasonable question, doesn't it? After all, we should have a logical reason for every decision we make. And I'm sure that you have all the time in the world to sit down and articulate that reason at your children's level of understanding every time they ask for it.

It's time to get ready for school. Sheri is dawdling and will soon be late. Mom says, "Sheri, hurry up and make your bed."

"But *why?* I'll just be sleeping in it again tonight."

"Sheri, put on a clean outfit."

"But *why?*"

"Sheri, we need to leave a couple of minutes early today, so hurry."

"But *why?*"

Now, I know that you would be delighted to stop for every one of those complaints and give a detailed explanation so that Sheri will feel much better about your requests. Yeah, sure.

John Rosemond, a parenting educator, describes "The Save-Your-Breath Principle": "Until a child is old enough to understand the 'Why?' of a parental decision, no amount of words will do. When the child is old enough, he'll be able to figure it out on his own. In either case, save your breath." He continues, "Today's parent seems compelled to provide explanations when children demand to know 'why!?' or 'why not!?' Despite the obvious fact that explanations serve no purpose other than a child's need to argue, parents continue to provide them" (*Daily Guide to Parenting*, Sept. 24).

This reminds me of our dog. Our dog has a bizarre habit. She is an "outside dog." In San Diego, that is no great hardship. But for the last twelve years of her life, she has been trying to dig through the glass of the back door. She stands up and claws and claws at the door. Not the brightest bulb. I think she is so dumb that she thinks if she digs hard enough, surely she'll be able to get through that glass door. Hasn't worked for twelve years, but by gum, she keeps trying. "E" for effort. "S" for stupid!

Children think that if they can argue enough, they can wear their parents down and win. They're very smart creatures. They will persist with the questions and demand explanations until they can get the parents to either give in or give up. And often, the parents do. For the kids, this is like gambling—if they think they have a chance of winning, they'll keep trying.

You will by and large make better decisions than your children will because you are an experienced adult. Take comfort in that. Don't feel like you have to explain everything. Say, "Because I said so" or "Because I'm in charge" or whatever strikes your fancy. But do not get sucked into this guilt trip. Take a vacation instead.

Watch out for walls

Don't create a wall for your teen to rebel against. Or if you do, make sure you pick it carefully.

My sister taught me this principle. Every teen has the

responsibility of separating from his or her parents. They start this as children and are really working on it hard as teens. If we set up lots of walls—lots of hard-and-fast rules—they will rebel against those walls as hard as they can.

This is crucial when it comes to the issue of the Church. You don't want that wall to be parent=Church. Kids need to rebel, or separate, from their parents. If you set up very strict, hard walls with the Church, then, to rebel against *you,* they also have to rebel against the Church because they perceive them as one and the same.

When your children try to rebel against Church things, pull out, *pull out,* PULL OUT! Most, if not all, of us will have this experience. When it has come up in our home, I have said: "Well, that is between you and your Heavenly Father, not me. Go and talk to Heavenly Father and let me know what He says." So if the issue was, "You force me to go to church. I'm not going!" you could say, "Well, that's not true. We want you to go to church. You go pray about it and let us know what you decide." Now, most of the time, this has worked well. Occasionally the child will make the wrong choice and stick with it. Again, *do not* get in the middle of this. I know this is excruciatingly difficult. I truly, truly know. I have siblings who have left the Church, so I know the danger.

But we cannot force our kids to stay in the Church any more than Lehi could or Alma could or Heavenly Father would. It must be their choice.

Knowing that, we need to not make withdrawing from parents synonymous with withdrawing from the gospel. You can pray, you can fast, you can bear your testimony often. But try as hard as you can to make the kids' spirituality their own deal.

They will test this again and again. Resist the temptation to jump on the wall. Now is not the time for your Samuel the Lamanite rendition. Sit quietly and assure them that their relationship with the Lord is their responsibility. You've taught them what's right and what's wrong, and it's up to them. Bear your testimony to them. And then step away. (And go hide on the other side of the wall and pray your little heart out. That's okay.)

If you set up lots of rigid walls, they will choose to run into them headlong. This doesn't mean you just give up on rules altogether. It simply means you're choosy about what walls you set up. And you can make them appear like one wall. For example, the rule in our home is, "We follow the prophet." That's a *big* wall in our house. When things come up, we compare them to that wall. Note that we do not have a "don't date until age sixteen" wall and a "don't listen to hard-core music" wall and a "don't watch R-rated movies" wall and a "don't swear" wall and on and on. If we did, the complaint would be, "You have so many stupid rules! I hate this!" Instead, we have one rule. It covers much, but it is still one rule and one wall. Their perception of that is much different even though the effect is the same.

The older the children get, and the more mature they are, the more you can take down the walls and give them the responsibility of building their own. Don't wait too long to hand over wall building. Begin at about age twelve and let them take responsibility for making good choices.

Occasionally, however, it's great to keep up a certain wall. Before I go into detail about this, though, I must stress that this is absolutely top-secret information. In order for you to read any further, you must raise your right hand and recite the parental pledge. Go ahead, stick your hand up. I'm waiting. . . .

Okay, recite after me: "I (insert name here—well, insert some good adjectives as well, such as I, the fabulous, intelligent, and charming Mildred . . .) do solemnly pledge that I will not reveal any of the following information to my children. And if my spouse is the yappy sort, I won't share it with him or her either." Okay, now we can carry on.

It is helpful to have a wall of sorts, one that I call, "The Parental Wall of Manipulative Rebellion." Boy, doesn't that sound important? Here's how it works. Recognizing that most kids need to rebel, pick something safe for them to rebel against and keep that wall up. For one of my kids, it is hair length. He spent his entire childhood with a buzz cut. He was adamant that the minute his hair was practically visible, it had to be buzzed. Well, all that has changed. Now he wants to wear it long. Longer than mine. So I make a big deal about it. My husband said, "Honey, just let this hair thing go." And I had to explain that this was our wall of the year. Now my son thinks he's being really rebellious by wearing his hair a little bit long. He goes around bragging to his friends what he's getting away with. Honestly, it is not that big of a deal to me. But whatever you do, don't tell *him* that! It's a very harmless rebellion that works out his need to rebel in some way.

My neighbor has his own wall. It's his son's sideburns. He confided in me that he and his wife really couldn't care less about their son's sideburns. (Frankly, I think they are *awesome* for a fifteen-year-old kid!) He said they just make a deal out of it so their son thinks he's getting away with something.

Is this manipulative? You bet. Does it work? Oh yeah. Just remember—maintain only *one* wall like this or you'll be doing damage to the relationship. Now, don't go sharing this state secret with just anyone. And whatever you do, don't tell my kids. Hmmm, don't tell my husband either. It still works with him.

You may think they're not listening—*but they are!*

My in-laws tell a very funny story about my husband. When he was a teen, they decided to start having family home evening. Now, that's an incredibly hard time to try to start such a thing, but I give them credit for doing it. My hubby spent those years hunched in the corner (*facing* the corner) or feigning sleep while being surly, uncooperative, and a general turkey. Later, while on his mission, he wrote a rather funny letter: "Dear Mom and Dad, Thanks for all those great family home evenings. I know you think I wasn't listening, but I was and I appreciate them."

This illustrates an important point. Even when we think our kids have totally tuned us out, they are listening. So it's very important to keep trying.

Talk short

The more important a topic is, the shorter our comments need to be. Kids have a hard time tuning into our long-winded dissertations. No matter how young or old they are, the minute they hear Mom or Dad winding up for a long one, they turn on their internal "mute" button (all kids were born with these) and go into that glazed-eyes, brains-elsewhere mode we are all familiar with.

It's far better to make a *very* brief comment and walk away. Whenever I remember to do this, my kids freak out. The minute I come toward them, I'm convinced they hit that "mute" button just out of sheer habit. So I make it short, "Son, whatever you do, don't do drugs." And then just walk away. They'll be stunned. "Whaaaa? What'd she say?" They come running after me, "What'd you say, Mom?" I turn and repeat and walk away again.

Those little comments stick with them. Often, we get a big laugh out of them. An ad will come on the TV and they'll say, "I know, Mom. Don't do drugs." And they laugh. But it sticks!

Short and sweet and don't repeat.

"Sweetheart, dress like a lady."

"Son, do your best."

"Honey, when you smile, you look absolutely beautiful."

"Jim, I'm proud of you."
"Carey, I pray for you daily."
And walk away.

Putting the Gospel in Their Lives

We've been taught over and over what to do to help our children develop spiritually. It amazes me, however, how much we ignore the basics. We must have them in place. Before we go any further, we have to commit to them.

At the minimum, every family must have daily family prayer and weekly family home evening. That's it, end of discussion. If we're not doing those things, we need to make every single superhuman effort possible to put those practices into place. They don't have to be picture-perfect, Norman Rockwellian events. For example, we have two family prayers in the morning because of seminary. Those who are up by then have family prayer in the car every morning at 5:30 before seminary so we don't wake the rest of the family. You don't see that picture—the family praying in the minivan in the dark—in any *Ensign*, but guess what, it works. And we do it every morning.

Much has been said on these topics by others, so I'll move on to other ways to help put the gospel into our kids' lives and hearts.

Go beyond the obvious

Ask yourself, what will help my child to feel the Spirit? Or, what will teach my child to feel the Spirit? To get the answers to these questions, you have to tune into the child. Each child is dramatically different from all others—the ways he or she experiences spirituality will be different as well. As we ponder and pray about these questions, we will be led to fine-tune our children's spiritual experiences to help them on a personal level.

One child may absolutely love nature, and that is how you can help connect that child to God. Talk about the Creation and the love and power of the Savior. Talk about animals and the love of family. Talk about birth and death and the plan of salvation. Help bridge the child's feelings to God by connecting those feelings with something that the child is keenly tuned to.

Other children may feel that connection through service. I'll talk more about that subject later in this chapter. Others may feel it through music. Buy lots of music! Talk about how it makes them feel. Help them feel the Spirit. One child may love to pray; another may love to teach. Give them lots of opportunities.

As you tune into each child, the Spirit will prompt you repeatedly to help you connect that child with Heavenly Father.

All children love to hear of the love of their Savior and the love of their Heavenly Father for them. Talk about this *all* the time. Recently my teenage son was struggling and, frankly, being a bit sassy. I looked him in the eye and said, "Son, I know that you are a good boy. And more than that, I know that your Savior loves you dearly. And I know that you know that He loves you. Don't ever forget that. He loves you so much He sacrificed His life for you." My son quieted and went away thinking. I don't care if they are four or forty-two, remind them often of how much they are loved. Remind them often of what was done for them personally. That, above all else, will help them connect to the Spirit.

Regular spiritual habits

The key to long-term success with a child's testimony is whether he or she develops regular spiritual habits. Now, honestly, we've had a struggle with this one in our family. And we're still working on it. But we are absolutely convinced of its importance.

There are various ways to work on developing these habits. Spiritual habits need to be guided by goals. I talked in the previous chapter about our white stocking full of "gifts for Jesus" and the goals on the walls of the kids' rooms. Setting spiritual goals will lead to the motivation to establish those habits.

There are several ways to help get these habits in place. Of course, the best way is to start when the children are small and help them pray and read the scriptures every single day. This takes absolute commitment on the part of the parents and is the very best way. But there is a transition that takes place when we turn these responsibilities over to the child.

You can work on this transition by using charts where the children track their own goal completion, "prayer rocks" (a rock placed on the pillow that you move to the floor when you've prayed at night, and then put it back on the pillow after your morning prayers), reminder posters, and so forth. All these reminders are helpful. As I've mentioned, we absolutely love using the giant white boards in the kids' rooms for them to remind themselves. Marking off a calendar can be useful as well.

Gentle reminders from the parents can help jog their memory. Help them go to bed early enough so they have time to read and pray before they are crabby and exhausted.

Here again, this is one of those areas that requires persistence. Also, we have to remember that after about age twelve to fourteen, it is up to them. Force has no part of the equation at this point and will only be counterproductive.

A huge part of having these regular spiritual habits stick is what kids see their parents doing. I teach seminary, and it's always interesting on parents' day at the beginning of the year when I talk about this. I talk about how every student is expected to read his or her scriptures for ten minutes a day and to pray every day. All the parents nod in agreement and support. Then I comment that the best way to accomplish this is for the students to see the *parents* doing this every day. Many of the parents start to examine their shoes carefully. How can we expect our children to master these things if we don't do them ourselves? I can't tell you the number of times I caught my mom in prayer by her bed or studying her scriptures. I can still see her with all the covers of her bed bunched up and Church books and her big scriptures all around her. That made a tremendous impact on my desire to become a scriptorian like my mom. It is no surprise that five of her kids and grandkids are teaching either Gospel Doctrine or seminary. Our children must see us doing the same things we expect them to do.

Now, it's perfectly okay to go to your child and say, "Honey, I haven't been setting a good example with scripture study, and that will change today. Would you read the Book of Mormon at the same time as I do? Then we can talk from time to time about what we're reading." That's a great example in repentance and commitment. Then do it!

Regular service for others

Service is a vastly underutilized method of spiritual parenting. It is also one of the most effective. All of us can point to experiences when we helped someone and came away filled with love and an increased understanding of our Savior. We need to give our children these same experiences.

President Gordon B. Hinckley has stated: "The antidote of selfishness is service, a reaching out to those about us—those in the home and those beyond the walls of the home. . . . A child who sees his father active in the Church, serving God through service to his fellowman, will likely act in the same spirit when he or she grows up. A child who sees his mother assisting those in distress, succoring the poor, and going to the rescue of those in trouble will likely exemplify that same spirit as he or she grows in years" ("The Environment of Our Homes," *Ensign*, June 1985, 3).

Teaching habits of service can start when children are very little. Make cookies and have the kids deliver them. Have them help you make a meal for a needy family. They can go help a senior friend or a disabled friend. We were extremely blessed to have a neighbor who was wheelchair bound. My children spent many hours reading their storybooks to her, reaching for things, helping with the dog, you name it. If you don't have a needy neighbor, *find* one! Emphasize to the children how much their help is needed and appreciated.

Recently we had a very powerful experience in our family. The Cedars Firestorm swept through the San Diego area. On Sunday, October 26, 2004, we saw the smoke and fires in our area. When we went to church that morning, we could see three huge fires burning. We were all sent home after sacrament meeting and advised to prepare for families needing to be evacuated. As we were watching the news, my son Brennan was on the phone checking on his friends in the areas being evacuated. Brennan came to my husband and me and said that his friends were being evacuated and that he and his friend Andrew were going to help them. We gave him water bottles, bandannas, and other supplies and sent him on his way.

As I watched the news further, it was announced that the Poway Community Center was the designated evacuation site. I told my family that I was going to go there to see if I could help out. My husband stayed behind with our two youngest kids in case our home needed to be evacuated. The kids went to work preparing the house in case we needed to house a family or to leave ourselves. I went to the evacuation center, which was in chaos. I worked with the Red Cross shelter manager, who designated me to be in charge of volunteers, donations, evacuee intake, and other concerns.

As I was helping at the center, I received many phone calls from Brennan telling me that his friends had been evacuated and that he and his friend Andrew were now helping fight the fires. I said, "How do the firemen feel about that?" He replied, "Mom, there are no firemen where we are. We just saved half a dozen homes."

Now, frankly, as a mom, that is not what you want to hear. But I had total faith that Brennan was a well-trained young man, an Eagle Scout, and I said a fervent prayer asking God to protect my son and keep him safe. I felt peace and knew that he was doing what he was raised and trained to do—serving others.

After a few hours, when it seemed that our house was not in danger, my husband brought our other two sons over to the evacuation center and then went back home to keep an eye on the house and to be available if it was needed for evacuees. Parker and Tanner worked hour after hour at the center helping tend evacuated animals, distribute food, and entertain the children.

Every few hours, Brennan and Andrew would come to the center to reload on water and face masks, eat a bit, and report what they were doing. They were covered in ash and had scrapes and cuts—and I've never seen them happier or more excited. Each time they came, they recounted to me the stories of the number of homes they had saved.

Brennan and his friend worked for hours and hours fighting fires on Sunday until well past midnight. During that time, I sent volunteers from the center to go help them, and they would work with Brennan for a while and come back to the center to tell of their exploits and homes saved.

The next day I went back to the center at 4:00 A.M. Parker and Tanner were up and ready. They wanted to go back and help. Brennan and Andrew got up early and went off to fight fires some more. It was a wild day again, but by the end of the day, they came back to the evacuation center to report that things were pretty much under control in Poway.

We kept the center open for four days, and all the boys worked like Trojans helping wherever needed. Throughout that time, many, many families came to the center to offer help. They came bringing their children, saying, "We want our children to be a part of this." And so we put them to work. We turned away many adults, but if a teen or a child came, we put them to work. I knew the power of service and that it would forever change their lives.

Later, I served as the Poway Fire Relief Coordinator, working with sixty-six families in Poway who had their homes burned down. It gives me such satisfaction to know that that number would have been much higher if it had not been for the heroics of my son Brennan. I am very, very proud of him. It was a frightening thing to participate in and know what Brennan was doing. But I knew that God watched out for him as he was working a miracle of his own to save many families from the heartache of losing their homes.

As a family, we worked for many months helping families with food, clothing, furniture, and housing. Day after day our porch would fill up with donated items, and my children would haul them in and then haul them out again as the families came by. It was an incredible experience for all of our kids to participate in feeding the hungry in a literal way.

We also participate as a family in a charity called Mothers Without Borders (motherswithoutborders.org), for which we make and collect items to be sent to orphans in Africa, India, and throughout the world. At every service project, we invite the children from the community to come. One time, we were assembling birthing kits to be sent to Bolivia, and several little girls were working with me. I asked them if they knew what we were doing, and they said they didn't really know. I explained how the kits were going to be used in the jungles of Bolivia to save mommies and babies. Each time one of them finished up a kit, I said, "You just saved a baby's life." They were shocked. They worked harder and harder and went home to tell their parents how many lives they had saved.

Experiences like that are priceless in helping a child to feel true love and a connection with their brothers and sisters throughout the world.

It's very easy to create these opportunities. The Church's Humanitarian Aid program is a great thing to participate in, and it's not just for the women. Get your kids involved! Have them crochet hats and make blankets. Show them pictures of kids from other countries who would receive these things. Take them to soup kitchens to serve and to nursing homes to practice their piano lessons. Take them with you when you donate blood, and talk about saving lives. Talk about the people they're helping when they go to the temple to do baptisms. Have them donate part of their allowance to charity, and talk about how it is used. Tanner was stunned to find out he could keep two children alive with just his allowance.

Teach them how their actions will impact generations. And teach them how to love and serve others by getting involved. Talk about the Savior and connect His love to those warm, wonderful feelings they will have. Get them in the habit of actively living as disciples of Christ would live. It will change their perspective in tangible ways and bless their lives forever.

Fasting, praying, and identifying answers

"A few years ago, Bishop Stanley Smoot was interviewed by President Spencer W. Kimball. President Kimball asked, 'How often do you have family prayer?'

"Bishop Smoot answered, 'We try to have family prayer twice a day, but we average about once.'

"President Kimball answered, 'In the past, having family prayer once a day may have been all right. But in the future it will not be enough if we are going to save our families'" (James E.

Faust, "The Greatest Challenge in the World—Good Parenting," *Ensign,* November 1990, 32).

It's always interesting to teach children. If you ask them if they've ever had an answer to their prayers, most will answer that they have not. A great spiritual parenting skill is to help them to identify when they get answers. This can be done by having family prayers and family fasting for a particular thing and then identifying the answer or blessing that is received.

Kids need to be taught to see answers in the blessings they receive. They don't always automatically connect the two. And sometimes, answers come in different ways from the ones they were expecting. That's why it is important to point those answers out. "Remember, we were praying that Daddy would get some good leads on a job? Well, he got three good leads this week. Isn't that wonderful that our prayers were answered?" "We were praying that we would know if our decision to move was the right one. As we think about that decision, we have a bad feeling. We feel Heavenly Father is telling us we shouldn't move right now." Be sure to identify these feelings you have and answers you receive.

A critical element is to help the children focus on the spiritual *feelings* they had in response to prayers and not always on "Did I get the puppy?" As we teach them to pray, we need to teach them to pause after they pray. We can show them how to stay on their knees and listen *deeply*. They need to be taught to tune into those feelings. So often, they pray quickly, jump in bed quickly, and fall asleep quickly, and then wonder why they don't get answers.

As important as it is to teach children to pray, it is just as important to teach them to listen for answers to those prayers. Ask them, "How do you feel when you pray?"

How does the Holy Ghost communicate with you?

One of the things a child needs to be taught is how to recognize communication from the Holy Ghost and the promptings that will come from Him. This understanding does not always come easily. Sometimes in Primary they will learn that people have a warm feeling when they feel the Spirit, and they may feel discouraged. "I don't have a warm feeling, so I must not be feeling the Spirit," they might think.

Once when I was teaching a group of investigators, I went around the room and asked them, "How do you feel when you feel the Spirit?" Each one had a slightly different answer.

"I feel a warm feeling."

"I feel cold and tingly all over."

"I feel a feeling of deep peace and calm."

"I feel a sense of clarity of thought—everything just comes into focus."

"I hear a voice, kind of like in my head."

"I feel awash in love."

"I feel goose bumps."

Each answer was unique to the person. Were any of them wrong? Of course not. But if we talk only about that warm feeling or about hearing a voice, others may not recognize that the Spirit may talk to them differently.

So teach this to your children. Ask them to tune into how they feel. Ask them to think back to a time when they felt strongly that the Spirit was with them, and have them describe it. Then reassure them that, over time, they'll grow more experienced in recognizing the Spirit.

These concepts need to be reinforced over and over and over. Understanding the Spirit is something we all struggle with. How much of what we feel and experience is from the Spirit, and how much is from our frenzied brain? We all go through these struggles. It's important to help our children as they deal with this and to share with them our own experiences. Most of all, help them connect to their own unique feelings and to gain confidence in their experiences with the Spirit.

Bearing testimony to them is #1

I saved the most powerful spiritual training technique for last. Go read in the book of Alma in the Book of Mormon, starting with chapter 36, where Alma is writing to his sons. This is a powerful example of spiritual parenting. Alma bears testimony to each of his sons in a personal and powerful way. And we know that this was successful because even his wayward son repented, and all his sons were true to the faith.

Bearing testimony is absolutely the most powerful spiritual parenting we can do. It is where the rubber hits the road. It is a personal witness that cannot be argued with or debated. Nothing except the child's own personal witness is stronger.

And yet this tool of testimony bearing is so rarely used. I think this stems from a lack of understanding and knowledge.

Missionaries understand the principle of bearing testimony. They use it in teaching investigators all the time. They know that as they are bearing a personal witness, the Spirit can reach out and testify of the truth of their words and bear witness to the investigator.

Well, guess what: Our kids are investigators, too! We need to treat them as such. They are investigators until they receive their own personal testimonies. This may come at age eight, or it may not come until age forty-eight. We cannot afford to be casual with our spiritual parenting at any stage.

As we teach principles and truths, we need to add our personal testimony of what we're teaching. It's one thing to have a lesson on the life of Jesus. It's another to have a lesson on Jesus that ends with Mom and Dad bearing solemn witness to the love of the Savior that they have felt in their lives and expressing their gratefulness for His atonement. The difference in the power of those two lessons is incalculable.

Bearing testimony can be simple. My mother often said, "I love the Old Testament. It speaks to my soul." There was a brief testimony borne right there. And I have fond feelings every time I read the Old Testament because my mother loves it so.

Testimonies should also be written down. I am an estate-planning attorney, which means that I prepare trusts and wills. One day an elderly couple came in to meet with me. The woman asked, "Can I write something to go in my will?" I assured her that she could. She said, "I want to put my testimony of the Savior in my will. It's the most important thing I'm leaving to my children. Much more important than the money we're leaving to them." She and her husband, both devout Lutherans, wrote beautiful testimonies to put in their will. They understood that they were leaving a legacy of faith to their children. What a gift to leave future generations! Take a minute to write yours down. This is very powerful spiritual teaching.

In the Book of Mormon, Helaman talks about his two thousand stripling warriors, who were such faithful young men and boys. One statement of those young men has always stuck with me, "And they rehearsed unto me the words of their mothers, saying: We do not doubt our mothers knew it" (Alma 56:48). They knew that their mothers had unshakable faith. They knew that their mothers had deep testimonies. How did they know that? They knew it because they had heard it from their mothers' lips. Their mothers had testified to them of their own faith and spiritual experiences. That led to deep bedrock, faith in their sons, who could rely on their mothers' unswerving testimonies.

I have pondered the idea of spiritual parenting for many years. I was listening to general conference in April 2003 and heard Elder Jeffrey R. Holland speak on this very topic in a powerful way. He said: "I think some parents may not understand that even when they feel secure in their own minds regarding matters of personal testimony, they can nevertheless make that faith too difficult for their children to detect. We can be reasonably active, meeting-going Latter-day Saints, but if we do not live lives of gospel integrity and convey to our children powerful heartfelt convictions regarding the truthfulness of the Restoration and the divine guidance of the Church from the First Vision to this very hour, then those children may, to our regret but not surprise, turn out *not* to be visibly active, meeting-going Latter-day Saints or sometimes anything close to it." ("A Prayer for the Children," *Ensign,* May 2003, 86).

Sometimes we rely on Primary, Mutual, seminary, and everyone else to convey these testimonies to our children. In fact, they are *our* children, and the most heartfelt testimonies they need to hear are our own.

Elder Holland continued: "Live the gospel as conspicuously as you can. Keep the covenants your children know you have made. Give priesthood blessings. And bear your testimony! Don't just assume your children will somehow get the drift of your beliefs on their own. . . .

"Do our children know that we love the scriptures? Do they see us reading them and marking them and clinging to them in daily life? Have our children ever unexpectedly opened a closed door and found us on our knees in prayer? Have they heard us not only pray *with* them but also pray *for* them out of nothing more than sheer parental love? Do our children know we believe in fasting as something more than an obligatory first-Sunday-of-the-month hardship? Do they know that we have fasted for them and for their future on days about which they knew nothing? Do they know we love being in the temple, not least because it provides a bond to them that neither death nor the legions of hell can break? Do they know we love and sustain local and general leaders, imperfect as they are, for their willingness to accept callings they did not seek in order to preserve a standard of righteousness they did not create? Do those children know that we love God with all our heart and that we long to see the face—and fall at the feet—of His Only Begotten Son? I pray that they know this" ("A Prayer for the Children," 86–87).

I add my prayer to that of Elder Holland. I pray that each of our children will know these things because he or she has heard them from our own lips.

Family Home Evening Planning

Family home evening is a sticky subject. Most of us either don't do it and don't want anyone else to know, or we feel embarrassed about the quality of our home evenings.

Well, take heart. Today is a new day. And if you have not been having family home evening, today is a good day to set that as your number-one goal. In fact, if you are not holding family home evenings, ignore the rest of this book and go do that. Remember, the Lord cannot bless you if you don't do what He says (see D&C 82:10). But if you do what He says, the blessings are enormous.

If you are among those who are diligently giving it their best shot week after week and are struggling with quality issues, take heart as well. I think to myself, "Well, our home evenings aren't quite as bad as Lehi's family!" Think about it. Some of their family get-togethers ended up with Nephi tied up and his brothers trying to kill him! Thank goodness ours aren't quite that bad yet. . . .

I remember planning a special family home evening for my oldest son, who was about to leave home to go to college. It was a "Salute to Connor" night. Well, things deteriorated quite rapidly. (In fact, I've noticed that there seems to be a direct correlation between the time and effort I have put into preparing a lesson and the speed with which the entire thing unravels.) Within a few minutes, somehow the entire brood ended up in a giant dog pile tussling on the floor, ending with Daddy doing a "Well, here I come!" and launching all 200-some-odd pounds of love onto the top of the pile. I sat there in shock. Connor peeked out his head from the bottom of the wrestling match and beamed up at me, "I'm sure going to miss this!" My heart melted.

So even if the activity portion of your lesson consists of a big family fight, keep your courage up! You're not alone!

Feeling versus content

No one can walk through the family section of a Church bookstore and not feel a serious guilt complex. All those books with all those pictures of perfect little families and all the planning, charts, diagrams, stories, and on and on! It's enough to wear you out.

I was feeling a bit discouraged one Sunday as I was sitting through a Relief Society lesson on family home evenings. Let's just say, *quality* home evenings have never been our family's strong suit. We have them regularly but, you know, they don't always sound or look that lovely. Anyway, the teacher made a comment that brought me up cold. I'll never forget it. She said, "Children may not remember everything you taught them, but they will remember how they felt." Then she repeated it.

That struck me right between the eyes. They will remember how they felt. They will remember feeling love, unity, fun, togetherness, faith, and warmth. They will remember feeling the Spirit. They may forget every story and every lesson, but they won't forget their feelings.

Suddenly, I realized that I was missing the point. There was no need to stress about having perfect choreography. We needed to feel family love and the Spirit. And that was enough.

Even if that love was felt in a giant family dog pile, it was okay.

Consistency is the most important thing

The prophets have taught that we are to have *regular* family home evenings and that if we do so, we will reap great blessings for our families. They do not say, "regular treats" or "regular visual aids" or "regular spectacular handouts."

The most important key to having successful home evenings (and consider carefully what "successful" means) is to keep trying. Week after week, year after year. Again, some experiences will be lousy, some will be memorable, some will be life-changing, some will be boring. The key is to keep trying. We will be blessed for our efforts—even just for trying. That's the beauty of it. And that's also the hardest part.

Family home evening packets

With all that said, I must admit that those groovy family home evening packets are worth their weight in gold. If you are unfamiliar with these, let me explain. You take a large envelope and put in it everything needed for a lesson, such as stories, visual aids, treat ideas, and so on. We have several large boxes filled with these, and so when it's time for a lesson, we can pull one out and start from there! They have been wonderful and have also helped with teaching assignments in Primary and Sunday School, talk preparations, and other uses.

Variety of methods and purposes

Family home evening changes all the time as your family changes. When the children are little, role-playing and story-telling are wonderfully captivating. As the children age, things change. Keep in mind that there is no one perfect teaching method. The key is variety. Try different things each week. Try different teachers, try different places, and mix it up.

We were having trouble engaging all the kids in our lesson when they got older until our friend Christa shared her family's solution: the "all contribute" method. They would pick a topic for the coming week, and everyone in the family had to bring something to contribute. They could bring a story, personal experience, scripture, or whatever. They could not repeat the same thing the next week, however, so if they brought a story the week before, this week it had to be something different. This really helped get all our teens involved, and the younger ones as well, and it improved the quality of the lessons tremendously.

But do not be afraid to do things differently. Some of our most powerful lessons have been in the Jacuzzi. Yup. The whole family in the Jacuzzi having a great talk. Maybe because it's hard to have a dog pile in a Jacuzzi . . .

Environment—Safe Haven

As I mentioned in chapter 7, we can accomplish lots of spiritual teaching with the environment we establish in our homes. We can use pictures of the prophets, temples, families, and scenes from scripture to establish a spiritual visual tone in our home. Music also plays an important role. The minute tension starts creeping into our home, I put good music on and the peace just flows. It's really hard to have a fight with that music playing!

You can also teach powerful spiritual lessons by what you *don't* have in your home. We teach one lesson by not having a single R-rated movie in our home. We don't have any trashy novels or magazines there either. I've had to end all my subscriptions to women's magazines because the headlines were so salacious.

We also don't have video games. There's just something about killing people and being excited and happy about it that rubs us the wrong way. Consider us old-fashioned, but death and mayhem just don't create the spiritual feelings we want in our home—not to mention the addictive, drool-infested comas kids waste time in.

Bottom line—we need to create a safe haven that says, "In this home, you are morally and spiritually safe." Children can know that, as with the temple, when they walk in that door, this is a home that is centered on Christ. Those feelings will stay with them forever.

Fill the Parental Emotional Tanks First

It's interesting to listen to a flight attendant describe what to do in an emergency on an airplane. They say that if the oxygen masks come down, "If you are traveling with a child, put on your mask first, and then help your child with theirs." Keep this in mind: oxygen first to the parent! A very important concept.

It is incredibly hard to help our children with their emotional development when we are drained dry ourselves. If the mother is dragging around like a beaten-up doormat, how can we expect the children to be emotionally healthy?

Look to your own emotional health—and look carefully. The most powerful lessons you teach your children are the ones you teach by example with your own life. Are you teaching them to take care of their health and get enough sleep? Or are you lurching through life sleep-deprived, overweight, and under-exercised? Do you teach them to take regular time off for fun and recreation? Or do you keep working, working, working, and grinding yourself to a pulp?

Remember, oxygen first to the parent!

"When He made babysitters, God intended for them to be employed on a regular basis. The full commandment is 'be fruitful, multiply, get a sitter, go out for the evening,'" says John Rosemond (*Daily Guide to Parenting*, Aug. 23). I believe that that is a true rendering of the scriptures! It is absolutely critical that we take care of ourselves or we will be of no use to our children.

The best parenting we can do is to adore our spouse. What a wonderful example, and, more important, what a tremendous foundation of love we give our kids. I gush about my husband all the time to my kids, and it drives them crazy. But I can see in their eyes how proud, happy, and grateful they are. And when we're smooching and they're rolling their eyes, I say, "Ah, you are *so* lucky! I'm married to a hunk!" Oh, they just die.

My siblings and I were taught in our home that mommies and daddies go out every week on a date. Our parents faithfully dated throughout their more than sixty years of marriage! This has been a powerful principle in our own marriages. My sister would tell her kids, "We're going out to fall in love again!" The kids would all chime in, "euwwww," but they had big smiles on their faces.

We need to zealously guard our spouse time. We must have a marriage-centered family to have a great base for our parenting. So hire that sitter and out you go!

As an attorney, I have seen many long-term marriages break up because the couple placed the children first in their family. All the time and attention was spent on the kids. So when the kids left, the marriage had nothing left. We must keep working on the marriage part of the equation, and that requires time—uninterrupted, unaccompanied-by-children time.

Make your children proud

We set powerful examples for our children. They watch everything we do. We can set a great example of achievement for them as well. They're proud of us when we're making our dreams come true. So work on your own dreams.

When I was growing up, my mom went back to school when her youngest child was in school. She worked for six long years and got her degree. I remember helping her with her homework and studying side by side. And I remember being so incredibly proud of her when she graduated. Any wonder I went to college and law school? Mom set the example of the importance of education.

Our friend Gary has become very well-off. (He'd be mad if I said he was wealthy.) He has used his money to establish a foundation that sponsors medical work in third-world countries. He and his wife are incredible, Christlike people. Any wonder their adult children are all involved and very charity-minded?

My sisters-in-law are both very creative and adept at crafts. They've set up a little business making pillows. I see how proud their children are of their moms' creative efforts.

It is very important that our children see us pursuing our dreams. Don't think you're being selfish. You are making a difference and setting a wonderful example for your children. You're teaching them invaluable emotional lessons as well.

If you respect yourself, they will be more likely to respect you as well. And if they respect you, they'll respect themselves because they have seen how to do it! That circular lesson sets the foundation for so much more. Don't deprive them of learning it.

Put the "Fun" Back in Dysfunctional

In the midst of all this angst over whether we're parenting well or messing it up completely, we're counseled to have fun. We could call this, "Getting in touch with your inner weirdo" or "Finding your happy place." Frankly, I'd like to move to my happy place. How about this one: "Having a paradigm shift right off the plane of normalcy," or we could even call it, "Discovering the Seven Habits of Highly Hilarious Families."

To test how you're doing on this, ask yourself, When was the last time your family had a gut-busting laugh together? If it's been too long, let's get on it! This is homework you can love.

All families have funny things they do. Our often-serious neighbor's family delights in dancing in their jammies in the living room. Another family has an annual Polar Bear Plunge into the frigid pool on New Year's Day. Some families play the Beatles at ear-piercing levels and sing along.

We have body part contests. (Heaven help my future daughters-in-law.) One day when we were sitting at Burger King, I said, "Who can wiggle their ears?" Well, it escalated from there, and pretty soon everyone was displaying what they could do with their very talented body parts. Parker won the day with a six-ruffled tongue folding that still leaves us mystified and impressed. This activity was so popular they used it at the Cub Scout pack meeting and it was a big hit. You should see the bishop's wife's tongue folding—wow!

Have fun. Stop the madness and run out and take everyone swimming. Go to Dairy Queen often. Sometimes when my dad was driving he would suddenly grip the steering wheel with stiff arms. "Hilda!" he would yell, "I can't control it!" We would all start giggling. "This car has a mind of its own! Here we go!!" and he would suddenly pull into the Dairy Queen or McDonald's for a treat. It was wonderful fun.

Those silly and delightful experiences will be treasured memories for your children as they pull them out and mentally review them. What priceless gifts they will have as they remember those warm bonds of love and family fun.

Remember that, as a parent, you have a priceless gift. You have the gift of the Spirit and are entitled to revelation for your children. As you help them develop emotionally and spiritually, tune in to that Spirit and be guided by it. Heavenly Father has known and loved your children for an eternity. He will help you as you strive to teach and train them. He's just waiting for you to ask for His help.

CHAPTER 9

How to Develop Parenting Skills and Mind-Sets

We've talked a lot about parenting, and hopefully you've gleaned some useful, practical helps along the way. To close with, I thought we'd chat a bit about some overall parenting philosophies and give you some skills to put into place to make the whole thing work better.

This chapter definitely requires some chocolates nearby, a big pillow, and your favorite slippers. So if you're ready, let's tackle the heady stuff.

Develop a Parenting Philosophy

What kind of parent are you? Are you strict? Creative? Organized? Spontaneous? Are you like your mom or dad, or *not* like your mom or dad? As you go through this parenting process, it is important to figure out what kind of parent you are. This will help you become centered as a parent in general.

Imagine this, if you will. You're a football coach. It's the first quarter and you are yelling at your team a lot, "Work harder!" "Jones, I've told you a million times to put that shoulder down." "This isn't a picnic; get to work!" Then, halfway through the first quarter, you call in the team for a quick chat: "You know,

I've been a bit hard on you. Let's just take it easy for a while. Let's be friends. What does everyone think we should do for the next play? Let's just vote on it." They walk away confused. In the second quarter, you shout, "You sissies couldn't play well if your life depended on it!" Then it's halftime. "Gee, guys, what was I thinking? Let's be friends. I'll pay for dinner afterward, my treat. Okay? Pals?" Third quarter: "I know goals have always counted for six points but now they're going to be only five. And no more penalties will be assessed for holding or interference." Then the final quarter comes and you change again: "No playing around. Dinner is off! Get back out there, and I want to see you play as hard as you've ever played in your life!"

Can you imagine a team playing well with a coach like that? They can't predict how the coach is going to act: authoritarian, permissive, wanting to be buddies, being mad as a hornet. And so they are caught, not knowing how to behave because the rules and conditions keep changing.

Orson Scott Card reported on a talk by Diana Baumrind, "Parental Discipline Patterns and Social Competence in Children":

"According to Dr. Baumrind's research, children of permissive parents, who get adult approval no matter how they behave, tend to be irresponsible. They depend on other people to make decisions. They learn no concept of right and wrong.

"On the other hand, Dr. Baumrind's research indicates that children of authoritarian parents, who are punished frequently without believing there is a reason for it, see the world as a hostile, unfair place, and they rebel—or give up in despair. In either case, they tend to be unable to adapt well to the adult world.

"Authoritative parenting tends to produce children who are able to think independently, who can make their own decisions, who, because they believe their own actions will decide whether good or bad things happen to them, are resourceful and self-motivated. They feel like a part of the world around them, acting as well as reacting.

"Of course, *authoritarian, permissive,* and *authoritative* are very broad terms, and there is no easy formula to follow. Furthermore, these studies show tendencies, not guarantees. Following the authoritative pattern of parenting does not guarantee that all your children will be more responsible, take more initiative, be more self-motivated—but it does improve the chances a great deal" ("Who's Minding the Children?" *Ensign,* August 1977, 9).

It's important to be centered and focused on your parenting mind-set so that the children have a stable situation to grow in. Does this mean we have to always be the same? Of course not. But our overall parenting framework needs to be in place. If we keep switching the rules, switching the consequences, and switching our reactions, the children will never be able to adapt.

Parents who have trouble honing in on a parenting philosophy are generally insecure and worried that something they do will cause lasting damage. Truthfully, most parents are doing a good job. Unless you are abusive, it is difficult to permanently harm your kids. Relax. Get comfortable with your role as parent. As you are more in control of yourself, your kids will relax as well. This takes some prayer and some pondering and studying as well.

How do you establish your parenting philosophy?

Consult "experts"

If you needed help repairing your car, where would you go for help? To a mechanic, of course. If you needed help with your computer, you would go to an expert—probably your twelve-year-old. When we need information or help, we go to experts.

Often parents wanting help will seek it out from child psychologists. Some of these are very helpful. But be careful with what you read. I always thought it was rather odd that so much credibility was given to child psychologists who trotted off to work each day—leaving their own children home with someone else—and then were the declared "experts" on parenting.

So turn to those true experts, the grandmas and grandpas and moms and dads and aunts and uncles who have real, on-the-job experience. Let's face it. The generation before us put out some pretty respectful children who were capable of taking care of themselves in the adult world. That's impressive. It's great to ask for their advice. Listen well. You will find yourself taking their advice more and more the older you get!

Friends and peers are also a great source of help with parenting. The hard part here is that we don't want to appear less than perfect. If they only knew—they might not like us anymore. Balderdash.

It's about time we set aside all that pseudo-perfection hooey and get real with each other.

Several years ago we had in our ward a family who was investigating the Church. They had been coming for a year and still had not been baptized. I was Relief Society president at the time, and the bishop asked if I would go over and have a chat with the woman, whom I'll call Ashley. Now, I thought the road-block to their getting baptized was tithing. Frankly, that has to be a tough principle to just start living. So I was yapping away about that. Nothing. We were chatting about other stuff, and finally an hour had passed. I said a little desperate prayer, but still nothing was forthcoming.

So finally I stood up to go and said, "Well, it's time to go back home to my little hellion. I so dread going back." She looked up at me sharply and said, in a timid voice, "You too?" At that split second the Spirit whispered to me, "That's it." I was thinking, "You have *got* to be kidding me." Nope, that was it.

So I said, "Well, yes. This child has been a royal pain since birth and it's really hard." She was absolutely stunned. I thought, *Oh, brother, I've really done it now.* After a full minute, she spoke up, "I can't believe I'm hearing this." I was now thinking it was time to backpedal vigorously. But she continued, "I've been having such a hard time with my son, Victor. I just keep thinking I must be a lousy mother."

"Oh, no," I assured her. I had seen her son in action and knew he had other demons he was dealing with. So I went on and described to her what it was like having a difficult child. She was nodding her head vigorously to every point I was making. I said, "He was sensitive and like this when he was a baby, wasn't he?" She replied that he was. I assured her that it had nothing to do with her being a lousy mom and talked about how to handle this type of child.

Then I continued, "Oh, Mary has one too—you know little Jared? And so does Kathy—you know Marietta?" and I named off several more. She was astounded. She said, "I had no idea you were all dealing with this. I thought I was a bad mother and unworthy to join the Church. You all looked like you were such perfect mothers and had such great families." I assured her that we were all grappling with similar issues and that the Church was full of moms working on their parenting just like her.

She told me later that as soon as I left, she called her husband and said, "Don, we can get baptized now. Now I know that I'm an okay mom just like the rest!" And sure enough, the whole family got baptized that week and have been faithful ever since.

And they had their son tested and learned that he had some physical and mental issues that needed addressing, and he's doing very well now.

Perhaps none of this would have happened if I was so paranoid about appearance that I didn't share the parenting struggles I was facing. Our peers can be wonderful allies and supports to us as we face our challenges—but not if we don't open up.

I have a group of girlfriends who have children of similar ages, and we go out once a month. Much of the time is spent discussing issues we're facing and how we're going about it. How reassuring that is! What great ideas they have! It is invaluable parenting support.

Be brave and start that support group going. Be open about what you're facing. It doesn't have to all be negative, either. Share the good and the bad. Be careful to protect those tender, private family things. But you can have great discussions about general issues that will be really helpful to you.

Of course the ultimate expert is our Heavenly Father. As I've said, He knows your children well and knows what will work. Consult Him regularly. Praying and fasting about your parenting challenges will result in whisperings and promptings to guide you. Be specific in your requests and He will answer you.

Trust your gut

Parents have incredible internal compasses to help them in their parenting. Learn to trust those feelings and inklings you have. Often they will come from the Spirit. Sometimes they will come from your past experiences and understandings you have gained. Rely on them.

A sweet mom I'll call Sharon related this experience to me: "I just had this nagging worry. It would not go away. I couldn't verbalize what it was, just a nagging sensation. I went and stood in my son's room and prayed. I moved some books around and there was a stash of some magazines."

I asked her, "What did you do?"

She said, "I called the school and said I would be pulling my son out of school and to have him at the office. I went and picked him up and he was rather belligerent. I didn't say anything until we got home. Then I sat him down and spread out the magazines. He turned pale and got really quiet. I spoke to him very softly. 'Son, I have had a nagging feeling for a couple of weeks now. Now I know that it was because the Spirit was prompting me to remove this evil from our home.' He asked me if his brother had told me and I assured him that he had not. We then had a long talk about how evil this was and what would happen next." I was so proud of my friend. She didn't dismiss those feelings. She trusted herself.

When your gut tells you something is off, perk up your eyes and ears. When your gut tells you you've made the right decision, stick with it. Learn to listen to that and trust yourself.

One time when I was a young mom, one of my sons got really sick. He was about eighteen months old and couldn't keep anything in his stomach. I took him to the doctor, who suggested a few remedies. The next day he still was sick and had lost a lot of weight. It was evening and I looked at him and had an overwhelming feeling. I called out to my husband, "We're going to the hospital *right now.*" We dropped off our other son and sped to the hospital. As we were driving, I told my husband, "I just can't shake this feeling that something is seriously wrong and he needs help immediately." So the first doctor came and looked at our son and said, "I think he'll be okay through the weekend. Why don't you bring him back Monday?" (This was Friday evening.) I said, "No, go get me another doctor!" So they went out to get another one. (Can you believe it!? I was only about twenty-five years old but pretty plucky!)

So in comes the next doctor and the same song. I said, "Get another doctor!" No lie. I went through *four* doctors! Finally, the fifth one came in. He walked over and said, "What's going on here?" Then he took one look at my son and said, "Nurse, get this child admitted immediately. He is severely dehydrated and needs an I.V. STAT." And so all the gears went into motion. He turned to me and said, "From now on, you ask for me. I used to be the head of pediatrics for a long time but gave up recently.

I'd had it with this system. So you ask for me and I'll make sure you're taken care of." After he left, I asked the nurse, "Why wouldn't the other doctors help us?" She said, "They don't like to have to monitor patients over the weekend." Well! That was certainly an eye-opener! Now, no offense to the fabulous doctors out there. But I learned my lesson: *Trust your gut!*

Be the parent!

I was donating blood once and heard the nurses talking. One said that her twelve-year-old son was going to the movies and that she thought there was a girl involved. Then she shrugged her shoulders, "Well, what are you gonna do? They're just gonna do it anyway." Of course, you know me by now—I piped up, "Gee, how about saying no?" She wasn't too happy with that.

Don't abdicate your parenting and just sit and wait for time to pass. We have to remain in control and be the parents. Just because it's difficult, time-consuming, and frustrating does not mean we just wilt and give up.

Perfect consistency is not necessary, but methodology helps kids feel stability. I find that if my child is being disobedient, I need to look at myself. The problem is often that I'm issuing threats and not carrying them out, waffling, changing, giving second chances, negotiating, and so on. Usually, we as parents are the ones who are not sticking to The Plan. We've become like that coach who is constantly changing, and so our children are waffling as well. When we step back and get ourselves firmly in control of our parenting, many of the discipline issues are resolved.

We don't have to administer the exact same consequence every time with every child. The important thing is that there *is* a consequence to disobedience. But what kind of consequence and how it is administered will vary from time to time *and from child to child!* Remember, we are learning as well.

Child #2 will pipe up, all indignant, "You didn't make Child #1 do this!" So you respond, "I know. We made a mistake in how we handled that and we're not going to make that same mistake with you!" "Why not?" they whine (remember Guilt Trip #2?).

You're not being inconsistent, you're sticking to your method: There will be a consequence for misbehavior. And you will change and improve and adapt to each child as you learn and grow as well. It's okay to be up front with that. "Jean, you respond differently to things, so we will handle this to fit you."

Now, sometimes behavior bugs us at one time and not another. Playing loud music in the morning may not bother you one bit, put playing that music at dinnertime may bother you a lot. We don't have to be consistently patient either. Kids know this. Also, some things will affect each parent differently. Kids know this, too. We don't have to be sticklers and say, "Well, dear, whenever the children do this, that must happen." Children know that their parents are different, and they don't expect them to always act the same. So we can let go of a lot of that concern and be ourselves.

But if we waffle between being permissive and then dictatorial and then back again, the children can't figure it out, and so they keep testing the boundaries.

Realize where it's coming from

Much of the misbehavior and difficulty we experience results from the fact that we're dealing with *children*. They are imperfect beings who mess up all the time. They are, after all, children; if they were perfectly capable, they'd have moved out by now.

But sometimes we get frustrated and think, "She should know this by now!" Well, you know you should study your scriptures daily—don't you? And you know you should eat better and exercise regularly—don't you? We are all learning and growing and making lots of mistakes. It helps if we keep a good perspective and realize that raising children is a messy process. Patience and more patience and even more patience will be necessary.

Realize—sometimes they're different

I was listening to a woman who had many children bear her testimony, and at one point she paused and then said, "You know, I've learned that a lot of times, what our kids do isn't necessarily wrong—it's just different." That stuck with me.

Sometimes our children just do things differently. Differently from the way we would do them, differently from how their siblings would behave, just differently. Not wrong.

That concept helps tremendously in gauging our reactions. Look at their behavior carefully and ask, "Is this wrong or is it just different?"

Once we have this theme—this parenting methodology—in place, then our children can fit their individual personalities into the framework of our family. It helps them govern their own behavior when they know that their parents will behave reliably. That provides a safe environment for the children, and they will behave much better.

Your discipline methodology is like your tool belt on which you hang your tools. You have your parenting mind-set that we've been talking about. Now it's time to hang some tools and skills on that and build your own parental tool kit.

Ten Tools for Treating Kids from Tots to Teens

1. Know who owns the problem

One of the hardest parts of parenting is feeling like you're carrying all of your kids' problems around like boulders in a backpack. You feel weighted down all the time. Well, here's your chance to unload!

Problem ownership asks the question, "Who is responsible for solving this problem?" If the answer is your child, oh happy day. Pull that rock out of that backpack and hand it back!

Parents carry around way too much responsibility for handling all of their children's problems. No wonder the kids never leave home. Why should they? Mom and Dad will take care of all their problems for them. What a deal!

Understanding this concept early will be a tremendous tool for helping to raise independent children.

If it's your child's problem, *do not own it*. Let the child take responsibility for solving it; you stay out of it.

So your sixth-grader calls and has forgotten her lunch. Repeat after me, "Not my problem." Your little one's favorite toy has broken, and he wants you to drop everything and go buy him a new one. "Gee, I'm so sorry. But that's not my problem." You could get used to this!

Now, the teen version of this expression is "Bummer!" Actually, this works well for all ages (and it works on spouses as well, but don't tell them I said that). So your teen forgot to prepare her talk and it's Sunday morning. "Bummer! Man, you must be worried!" Note, at no time do you say, "Oh, well, let me just write up something for you to read." None of that! Who has responsibility here? She does, not you!

Try it some more. It's Monday morning, and your son is whining, "Moooommm, my P.E. uniform is still dirty." "Bummer! You must feel bad you didn't get it washed in time."

If you can learn this one concept, you will add ten years to your life and eliminate about 1,000 gray hairs. If it is their responsibility, let them own it. Do not bail them out. Do not fix it. Do not take it over and solve it. Let them own it.

What's great is, you can be supportive, empathetic, loving, and still let them have the responsibility. "Oh, honey, I am so sorry about this. I know that's got to be frustrating. But I know you're good at solving problems, so you'll handle this."

Now, when you first try this, all heck will break loose, so brace yourself. Your children will look at you in complete horror. "What?! You're not going to wash it (make it, buy it, solve it, pick it up, drop it off, whatever)?!" They will be filled with righteous indignation. They will try everything in their Kids' Arsenal of Guilt Trips. Be prepared.

Realize that the single biggest attribute of independent people is that *they can solve their own problems.* So let them! And often!

"Not my problem," or "NMP," as we call it, will change your life. I have parents write me from all over the country that this single change in their parenting was the most effective. So give it a try. And don't back down. Remember, you are giving your children a great gift.

2. Listen actively (when it is *their* problem)

Now, I know you're a little shocked by our first parenting tool, and you're asking what you *should* do when it's their problem. The key here is to actively listen. Listen without reacting, questioning, or interrupting. In fact, the best response is "hmmmm" or some other mumble. Excellent!

Let them talk; let them rant; let them cry. And then respond by mirroring their feelings back to them, "So you're feeling upset because your P.E. uniform is dirty." And then they'll vent some more, and if you keep listening, they will bridge to the real issue: "The kids will make fun of me and this one kid always does and he's being really mean to me." And so you give the active listening response again, "So you're afraid of this one guy." "Yeah, you should have seen what he did last week . . ." and away you go.

It never ceases to amaze me how, when I stop and shut my yap and listen carefully, my kids will open up. And often we end up in a completely different place from where we started, and we can get to work on the real underlying problem that is troubling the child.

If I had jumped in and solved the problem for them, we would have never gotten there at all.

A great discussion of active listening and the following tool, I-messages, can be found in *Parent Effectiveness Training in Action* by Dr. Thomas Gordon (Bantam Books, 1976).

3. Use I-messages (when it is *your* problem)

When we have a problem, the best way to bring it up with the person is through the use of I-messages. They go as follows:

"I feel (fill in feeling) when you (fill in what the person is doing) because (fill in the impact it's having on you.)"

For example, "I felt embarrassed when you didn't clean the bathroom because I had a client who needed to use it and it wasn't clean." These statements are hard to argue with—who can deny that we have our feelings and we are being affected? Plus this approach keeps the shields down. If we say, "You knucklehead! You didn't clean the bathroom and my client needed to use it and it was disgusting." Okay, by the time you uttered the word *you,* your child had put up a defensive shield and nothing much else got through. You've seen it happen. The minute you start in, the kids instantly clamp shut.

When you start with "I" and describe how *you* are feeling and reacting, they are more open. "I was exhausted and worried when you came home late last night because I had to stay up to make sure you were okay and I have to teach seminary in the morning." Direct impacts, real feelings.

Now, this can backfire, so we need to be careful. We must be sure that the child's behavior truly does affect us, or this will not work. Try this, "I'm . . . mad . . . when you don't cut your hair because . . . I'm embarrassed." Sorry, didn't work. Try that again and fill in how it directly affects you—and good luck. Hair is a tough one. So is cleaning their room! (To which they reply, "Shut the door.") You can't fudge a real I-statement.

When it's a valid situation, the power of phrasing your needs this way is immeasurable. Says Dr. Gordon: "Many parents were also surprised to discover how often their kids demonstrate a willingness to help, once they're told that their parents are hurting. And parents were amazed at the ability of their children to find creative and appropriate solutions after learning they had been causing their parents a problem" (*P.E.T. in Action*, 141).

4. Negotiate (when the problem belongs to both of you)

When both parent and child have a problem, sometimes negotiating can be helpful to mediate a solution. This is particularly true as the children get older, although this can be used with younger ones as well.

Begin by stating the problem and coming to a consensus so you agree on what it is. Then you can ask for suggestions as to solutions from the children, and come up with some of your own as well. Don't react at this point to the kids' solutions, and don't let them react to yours. Just say, "We're coming up with some ideas, so let's just put them all out there."

Discuss and negotiate which solution you will try. If you can't come to an agreement and commitment from everyone, keep going through the alternatives until you do. For little ones, you can lay out the choices yourself. You can say, "Well, we can either take your bath the night before, or lay your clothes out, or get up earlier. Which one do you think will work?" You are training them in the art of negotiating, and this will be a wonderful skill for them to have for the rest of their lives.

Be careful, though. As they get older, they get to be *really* good negotiators!

After you agree on a solution, also decide on when you will

come back together to see if the solution worked. This evaluation step is crucial. So many times, a solution is not working and things bog down and the problem is not solved and time goes on. It's best to decide in advance when you'll get together to see if that solution worked, if it needs some fine tuning, or if you need a new one altogether.

Let's run through a scenario so you can see how this works. Suppose that making lunches has turned into a headache. The children are complaining about the content of the lunches but they're not getting up early enough to make them themselves. You're having to nag them, and you aren't getting a good shopping list from them so you can buy what they want. This is a problem for you and the children.

So you sit down with all the kids and say, "O loved ones, let us converse." You know, sometimes I really do talk like that to the kids. It messes with their heads. And honestly, those kids have really developed excellent vocabularies! Ha!

Anyway, you're all sitting down in front of the giant white board or the pad of paper or whatever. You say, "We have a problem with the lunches." Now everything goes crazy as they all start talking: "You bet we do. I didn't have time to make one today and I'm starving to death." "Yeah, all the other moms make their kids' lunches. Why don't you?" "That cheese stuff you got last week for us was gross. Even the dog wouldn't eat it."

Try to rein this in a bit. "Okay, so the lunch arrangements need some work. Let's talk about some suggestions on how to fix this." Let them come up with the first suggestions and list them on the board—without comment!

"Mom should make them all."

"Mom should buy those cool Lunchables for every day."

"Mom should give us the money to buy better stuff at the store."

You will note that all of the suggestions will be aimed at you. Let's be realistic. They think that any problem is your problem. Okay, so you can begin to add some of your own.

"Children should get up half an hour earlier to make their own lunches."

"Kids should submit wish lists for shopping a week in advance."

And on and on you will go.

Then you can discuss all of these and see which will work and which will not.

Now, what's interesting is that you may not always come up with the same solution. When we addressed this problem with our children when they were younger, we ended up going with the suggestions of getting up earlier and submitting the wish lists. But when the kids got older, they asked to have this matter rene-gotiated. They came ready. They wanted to negotiate buying lunches at school all the time. I immediately said that that would cost too much money. They asked to have the opportunity to argue their case. Do you know those little smarties had an entire cost analysis done showing that by the time we calculated in the time I spent shopping, the cost of food, and all other factors, we were saving only ten cents per lunch! I was shocked. So we decided to give buying lunches a try, and it has stuck for the last five years! Not only that, my children love salads (okay, I know that's a bit weird) and they eat them every day as part of their lunch.

So be prepared for different alternatives, and let them prove their case.

This negotiating tool is also very useful for mediating between children. Sometimes at our house we set it up like a court and they have to each present their case. We'll have the other kids sit as a jury and I'm the judge. It's very effective. And it could also explain why they are now all so danged verbal and skilled at negotiation and argument. Whew!

5. Say it and *mean* it

You're at the grocery store and your three-year-old pitches a fit and starts demanding cookies. You say, "Be quiet, sweetie." She escalates. "Honey, be quiet because you're disturbing the people in the store." She gets louder. "Charlotte, pipe down right now or you'll be in trouble!" Kicking ensues. "I mean it, if you aren't quiet right this minute, I'm going to take you home." Now she starts flailing and wailing louder. "I said, I mean it, be quiet right this *instant,* or I will take you home!" She has now reached ballistic proportions.

What do you do?

You pull her out of the cart, go tell a checker that you won't be back for your groceries and you're sorry about that, walk out to the car, put her in, and drive her home. Then you put her in her room and tell her she can rant all she wants to in there. You look her right in the eye and say, "If you ever do that again in a store, I will take you home again and you will not get to play with your friends or watch TV or do anything else for the whole day."

Now, most parents cave in and buy the cookie. By doing so, they set up a training that is indelibly imprinted on the child's mind: "If I make a big enough fuss in a store, I will get my way."

Say it and *mean* it. Don't waffle, don't explain, don't hesitate. Say it and *mean* it. The more you can pull that off, the more you will imprint on your child's brain, "Well, he really means it on this." And that is wonderful training that will save you untold headaches for years to come.

6. Set your kids up

As a child, I was extremely upset about new situations. They terrified me. I've seen my kids react in various negative ways to new situations as well. A lot of pain can be avoided if we set up our children by explaining in advance what is expected of them or what is to be expected to happen.

So you're heading off to your sister's house for Christmas Eve. Beforehand, you say to the kids, "We're going to go to Auntie's for dinner on Christmas Eve. We will be wearing nice clothes like you would wear to school. We will be eating dinner there, so we need to use good manners. After the dinner, we'll be having a story time and sing-along, so we need to all participate and have a good attitude. Please spend some time talking to Granddad. Remember to thank Auntie when we leave. We'll have no fighting whatsoever. If you need to run around, you need to go outside. If you misbehave, we will take you out to the car and you will miss desserts and the Christmas treat." This will do wonders in eliminating frustration and misbehavior. Now the kids know what is going to happen to them and what is to be expected.

Another twist to this is to warn children when you're not doing well for some reason. If you are not feeling well, frazzled due to other things, hormonal, or whatever, it's good to give the kids a heads-up. We used to have a little sign hanging on the fridge that said, "Mom's mood" and had hooks for "Great," "Good," "Fair," and "Watch out!" There was a little heart on a string that you could move to the appropriate hook. I thought it was cute and would move the heart around, but eventually I grew lazy. One day, I happened to glance at the sign and realized that the heart was on "Watch out!" I laughed and asked who had moved it. One of the kids looked guilty. I said, "Hey, good idea." So from then on the children would move the heart back and forth according to what they observed in me, and occasionally I would move it as well.

Children often internalize and blame themselves for reactions that have nothing to do with them. Maybe we've got a headache, or we're worried about something, and it has nothing to do with that child. But they get the reaction. It saves a lot of grief if you can just say, "You know what, I'm not feeling so hot today, so let's just cool it." Instantly, they can react to that and tread easier. At least, that's the hope!

7. Call a time-out—for parents as well as kids

We're all familiar with time-outs. These are a great tool for parents and should not be limited to toddlers. Sometimes kids, and parents, need space. Use that space to cool off or just to have time alone. As a mom, I take lots of time-outs. I say, "Well, I need to give myself a time-out because I'm a bit frazzled right now." Off I go to my bedroom to cry, ponder, pray, read, sleep, or whatever I need. When the children were young, I'd leave the door open and they would stand there wide-eyed. I'd say, "Don't come in! Mommy's having her time-out!"

Families bump into each other a lot. Give the kids space to work things out . . . and give yourself space as well.

8. Have your spouse handle it

Often parents try to go it alone and end up going in circles. Using both wings of the airplane provides balance. Sometimes the best solution is to step back and let your spouse handle it! In fact, the older my husband and I have gotten, the more we've learned to take turns. I'll say, "Well, I was bad cop last week, so it's your turn this week." And then I step back and let him handle it. Or he'll come to me and say, "I'm really having a conflict with him. Can you take over on this issue?" And a fresh parent can step in and help resolve it.

Both parents have unique gifts. One is typically, by nature, more easygoing than the other. Treasure that balance and don't fight it! Let him handle it and don't question his methods. His methods are different from yours. Yahoo! What a blessing! Let him be different from you. It's okay.

If you're single, you handle one side and then pray to Heavenly Father to handle the other, and He will.

9. Use other people

Our teaching, training, and parenting don't all have to be done by Mom and Dad. There are lots of other people in our children's lives, and we can use them to help. Teachers, advisers, priesthood leaders, neighbors, relatives, you name it! If you're needing help, go to them. Ask them. Be specific about what you want from them and what they can do for or with your child. They are often happy to step in. And frankly, we could all use help and support!

10. Aim for clarity

Sometimes conflicts between parent and child can be caused by simple misunderstandings. To avoid these, try to be clear and precise on the level of the child's understanding. One day I was helping to set up a new Boys and Girls Club in our community. Many people were helping, including a young boy. I handed him a big, empty box and said, "Mike, would you put that in the hall, please?" He gave me a blank look. "What's a hall?" he asked.

We sometimes assume that children understand something when they do not. Or we assume that we have given clear directions when we have not. When kids question, we can ask, "Can I make that clearer?" This may seem repetitious or monotonous to us, but it will help to communicate in a way that's not misunderstood.

And if these misunderstandings do arise, by all means, have a sense of humor about them.

And our bonus tool—laugh!

You have to keep a sense of humor as a parent or you'll never survive. Well, maybe you will, but you'll be miserable! Laugh at yourself. Laugh at the funny situations you end up in. Don't take yourself or your parenting too seriously. Often my kids will say, "Mom, you're weird!" I always answer, "Why, thank you! I try so hard to be weird, and that's a fine compliment!" So one day my son's friend is over and he teasingly says, "Your mom is a little bit weird." All the boys chime in, "Don't say that! That's her favorite compliment! She loves that!"

Feel free to poke fun at yourself, your kids, your odd family, your weird habits. A light heart will make things much more bearable.

Be a Confident Parent

"As a parent, you'll never be perfect, but you'll always be the only mother or father your child will ever want," says John Rosemond. "Take that as a vote of confidence and do your best, because your best is always and forever going to be good enough" (*Daily Guide to Parenting,* Dec. 30).

I know that you wake up every day wanting to be a good parent. I know that you pray diligently for help in raising your children and that you are trying to do your best. Not one day do you wake up and say, "Well, today I think I'll be a lousy parent." Never happens.

So take confidence in that. Know that you're doing your best every day. Count on your Heavenly Father to make up the difference. He will.

Every parent reading this is willing to stand against the fires of Satan and against the raging of the world. So trust yourself and trust the Spirit.

I've loved chatting with you. Don't worry, you're doing a great job. And they'll turn out fine.

index

About the Author

Merrilee Browne Boyack is a crazed woman who loves eating ice cream and taking naps when she can. A professional lecturer and a popular speaker at BYU Education Week, she has taught parenting principles to thousands. She is an estate-planning attorney who conducts her part-time law practice from her home in Poway, California.

Merrilee graduated with high honors from Brigham Young University with a degree in Business Management—Finance and was a summa cum laude graduate from the Santa Clara University Law School. She has four sons and a fabulous, supportive husband. She is public relations spokesman for the Boy Scout San Diego Imperial Council; vice president of the local chapter and national board member of Mothers Without Borders; a member of the Poway City Council; community chair of the Boys and Girls Club of Poway; Rotary and Poway Chamber of Commerce member; and a community activist. She received the BYU Alumni Association Community Service Award and the PTA Council and Unit Honorary Service Award.

Merrilee's favorite kitchen appliance is a telephone. Her interests include reading, camping, talking, eating out, and riding her motorcycle. (See Merrilee's Web site at Boyacks.com or contact her via e-mail at maboyack@gmail.com for more information.)